TAKE  THE FLAG

FOLLOWING GOD'S SIGNALS IN THE RACE OF YOUR LIFE

ROB FUQUAY

ENLARGED-PRINT EDITION

UPPER ROOM BOOKS®
NASHVILLE

Cover design: Marc Whitaker/MTWdesign

Interior design: Perfect Type, Nashville, Tennessee

Library of Congress Cataloging-in-Publication Data

Names: Fuquay, Rob, author.
Title: Take the flag : following God's signals in the race of your life / Rob
   Fuquay.
Description: Nashville : Upper Room Books, 2017.
   Identifiers: LCCN 2016006364 | ISBN 9780835815826 (enlarged print) |
ISBN 9780835815796 (mobi) | ISBN 9780835815802 (epub)
   Subjects: LCSH: Christian life. | Spiritual formation. | Automobile racing—
Religious aspects—Christianity.
   Classification: LCC BV4501.3 .F86 2017 | DDC 248.4—dc23
   LC record available at https://lccn.loc.gov/2016006364

Printed in the United States of America.

I dedicate this book to my parents,
Bob and Julie,
for establishing my race of life on the values of
honesty, humility, and hard work
and who continue to show me
how to run well and finish strong!

CONTENTS

YOU'RE IN THE DRIVER'S SEAT

I may be going out on a limb here, but if the apostle Paul were alive today, I think he'd be a big fan of car racing. Why do I say that? Because Paul had an obvious fascination with the racing of his day. In his first letter to the Corinthians, notice the way he illustrates the spiritual life: "Do you not know that in a race the runners all compete, but only one receives the prize? Run in such a way that you may win it" (9:24). He often spoke about the race of faith. And look at how he sums up his life in his letter to Timothy: "I have fought the good fight, I have finished the race, I have kept the faith" (2 Tim. 4:7).

There's no doubt Paul witnessed footraces, and obviously he saw a larger meaning in them. In this day and age, when life moves at breakneck speed, why wouldn't Paul be attracted to the thrill of car racing? I know I am and, like Paul, I can easily see symbolism in this modern-day sport. Auto racing can help us describe our lives.

One day we will cross a finish line. The engines will stop. But what are we racing for? The aim of this book is to help us think about that question.

I didn't start out as a car-racing fan. I was five years old, growing up in North Carolina, when I went to my first race with a friend whose dad was a big fan. All I remember of that experience was clamping my hands over my ears, trying to block out the roar of the engines, and then having a headache that lasted three days. Not exactly the way to make a kid fall in love with the sport.

Yet all that has changed since I've served churches in the two biggest auto-racing cities in America: Mooresville, North Carolina, and now Indianapolis, Indiana. Mooresville is about thirty miles north of Charlotte, which most people consider the home of the National Association for Stock Car Auto Racing—of course more popularly known as NASCAR. Yet Mooresville is where most of the NASCAR race teams locate their garages and offices, and many drivers live in the surrounding area of beautiful Lake Norman. A Mooresville water tower declares it's "Race City USA!"

During my time there I got to know drivers, team owners, and people involved with various aspects of racing, such as crew teams, mechanics, and suppliers of car and engine parts. I learned more about stock-car racing and began attending races. From Mooresville I moved to Indianapolis, which, of course, is known for one of the biggest racing events in the world, the Indy 500.

It's easy to tell the difference between IndyCars and stock cars. IndyCar features open-wheel racing; their wheels extend outside the car body. The wheels on stock cars are located under the fenders.

IndyCars go significantly faster than stock cars because of their light weight and low-to-the-ground design.

There's lighthearted jesting between fans of the two series. After I moved to Indianapolis, a new friend gave me a greeting card that depicted two guys in ball caps and overalls standing by a shiny automobile. Below it was the caption, "Ever wonder how NASCAR got its name?" Inside the card one fellow says to the other, "That's a nasss car. Yep, that's a real nas-car." I got a good chuckle out of my friend when I read it aloud with my own Southern drawl.

Over the years I've grown in my appreciation for car racing and all the traditions that go with it. One that especially intrigues me is the sport's use of flags to send signals to the drivers. It's amazing to think that, for all the sophisticated engineering that goes into today's cars, the racing world still sticks with this age-old form of communication. The use of flags in competition can be traced to bicycle racing in France in the 1860s, and they became a common sight when car racing was born in the 1890s.

Historians have tried unsuccessfully to trace the origins of racing's most famous flag, the checkered flag, but they speculate that perhaps someone improvised with a checkered tablecloth to signal the end of a race. Other flags eventually came along to send different messages to the drivers: start, yield, caution delay, disqualification, final lap. However the use of flags began, they're obviously practical. Early racing, especially, was a dusty affair, so drivers could see the flags through the haze. Flags also speak boldly amid the deafening noise of the race.

It's no giant leap to garner greater understandings from this symbolic form of communication. God too is signaling to us amid the bustle and noise of our fast-paced lives. As I reflected on the racing flags, I began to see how their messages correspond to the important moments in our spiritual lives as God seeks our attention. And so in this book I will be using the flags of car racing as a jumping-off point to discuss different aspects of faith:

The Green Flag (start): How do we start our journey of faith?

The Yellow Flag (caution): Our life decisions can put us in peril on our journeys. How do we learn to heed God's cautions along the way?

The Blue Flag (yield): All of us may run our own race, but it's also essential that we respect others. How does God help us focus on other people's needs?

The Red Flag (delay): When life throws us unexpected and unwanted interruptions, how does God help us get the most out of these stops?

The Black Flag (disqualification): What happens when our own violations take us out of the race, and how does God help us get back in?

The White Flag (final lap): As we head to the finish line, how do we steer according to God's will?

The Checkered Flag (victory): If we persevere—navigating the hazards, managing the pit stops—then victory is ours. But how does God want us to experience victory?

If you are a racing fan, I hope this book will give you new appreciation for your race of faith. Even if you are not a race fan, I hope you find relevance in the meaning behind the symbolism.

I wrote this book not to make you into a racing fan but a greater follower of Jesus Christ, the author and perfecter of our faith. Just as God sends us signals, Jesus holds the key to the ignition of faith.

But that still puts you in the driver's seat. So buckle your seat belt, strap on your helmet, and in the words of NASCAR announcer and former driver Darrell Waltrip, "Boogity, boogity, boogity, let's go racing!"

THE GREEN FLAG

Let the Race Begin

Romans 10:5-13

The first NASCAR race I attended was the Coca-Cola 600 in 2008. This race, held every year in Charlotte, North Carolina, is run on the same day as the Indy 500. I knew auto races could be really loud (remembering my experience some forty years before), but for this one, I would be joining church members in an enclosed suite. I figured it surely wouldn't be as noisy as in the stands.

While the drivers took their warm-up laps, I turned to my friend and said, "This isn't as loud as I thought it would be." He nodded knowingly and said, "Wait until they wave the green flag." I thought, *The cars are already running. How much louder could it really get?* Then the green flag was waved. Honestly, I *felt* the difference before I heard it. My seat started shaking, and the walls vibrated. Then it came: the deafening roar. There was no point in even trying to speak. No one could hear a word I'd say.

Until the green flag appears, drivers leisurely move around the racetrack, maintaining positions that have been determined by their qualifying runs. But the green flag changes this coasting into a full-throttle, earth-shaking experience. As long as there are no caution flag, delays, or halts, a race continues "under the green flag" until the very last lap. This means drivers are free to reach top speed. A green flag signals that the race has begun.

Now, think about this image in relation to the spiritual life. If you are a person of faith, have you ever felt as though you were just coasting, driving warm-up laps? Nothing is wrong. You wonder why your faith doesn't have more energy and power. Or perhaps your faith life consists mostly of practices and routines that make you feel like you're simply going through the motions. You are looking for something more dynamic, something that will make a difference in your life and in the world around you. Have you ever wished someone would wave a green flag of faith that takes life from coasting to a full-throttle, earth-shaking experience?

As you think about that question, it's crucial to understand what we mean by faith, and specifically the Christian faith, since this will be the baseline for all we talk about in the following pages.

Defining faith shouldn't seem all that complicated. We all have ideas of what it is, but I suspect we formed some of those ideas in childhood when our difficult questions may have received easy answers. So it's equally important to understand what faith *is not*. Faith isn't a feeling or a proposition to believe. It's not religious knowledge or an endless list of good deeds to be done. That's not to say doctrine and works are unimportant. Or that rituals, symbols, and traditions have no significance. By no means! Yet without something more living and dynamic, faith is pointless. John Wesley, founder of Methodism, described this kind of faith as "having the form of religion but not the power."

So what is faith?

First, faith is a trust—a trust in a reality that has yet to be fully realized. That reality entails more than a belief in heaven. It informs a confidence that one day there will be heaven on earth, that someday the kingdom of God will arrive, and life will become what God intends it to be. Hebrews 11:1 puts it this way: "Now faith is the assurance of things hoped for, the conviction of things not seen." Interestingly, the Gospels use the words *kingdom of God* and *kingdom of heaven* interchangeably. They don't describe a place so much as a way of life, life as it looks when God's reign is in full effect. As far removed as that way of life seems at times, faith holds on to the possibility that one day God's way of justice and mercy will be in effect.

Faith also is action: stepping out in trust. In Genesis, we read about Abraham—the father of the Jewish, Muslim, and Christian religions—leaving behind his native country and everything familiar to him to go to a new land because he trusted in God's will and purpose. Faith is moving to the place where we give full control to God's direction. In this sense, it is more verb than noun. Faith is trusting in God's picture for our world and actively moving toward it.

So *Christian* faith means trust and action have a name. We trust that God's ideal way of life is embodied in the person of God's son, Jesus Christ, and we show that trust by following his teachings and example. The apostle Paul wrote his letter to the Romans to define what it means to live out Christian faith. The recipients were people for whom faith had become a matter of coasting along by following rules and rituals. Paul said the way to turn faith into a full-throttle experience was to take the green flag!

Well, not in so many words. But he did say that turning faith into an experience of energy and excitement requires going to the starting line. What is that? Just this, says Paul: "If you confess with your lips that Jesus is Lord and believe in your heart that God raised him from the dead, you will be saved" (Rom. 10:9). In essence, the green flag of Christian faith is accepting Jesus Christ as Lord and Savior.

Okay, before stepping on the accelerator, let's pause for a moment. Just as we defined faith by first saying what faith is not, let's do the same with this statement. For some, the expression "accepting Jesus Christ as Lord and Savior" rubs the wrong way. It takes people back to altar calls or invitations of faith that felt forced, coerced. Perhaps you have your own experience of worship services or camp settings where a preacher or some leader told you the words to say, regardless of your questions. I know some people who succumbed to this pressure for fear of rejection by family and church members.

For other people, accepting Jesus Christ as Lord and Savior reminds them of a simplistic, other-worldly focus. "Is your life a mess? Are things not right? Just accept Jesus as your Lord and Savior!" *Hocus-pocus, everything will now be fine because you've said the magic words.* It's even easier than Jack's beans and a lot less work than climbing the beanstalk!

In my own life I've had people tell me that accepting Christ as Lord and Savior means all kinds of things, from speaking in tongues to never having any doubts in my faith. Really? No doubts? Speaking in tongues? You can imagine the second-guessing this caused me, particularly during my adolescence. At times I felt like a teenage faith wannabe. Thankfully, years of spiritual growth, good faith friends, mentors, and my understanding of scripture helped dispel some of these ideas. But that still leaves us with an important question . . .

What does accepting Jesus Christ as Lord and accepting Jesus Christ as Savior really mean? Let's consider those positions one at a time and start with the second first.

What Does It Mean to Call Jesus *Savior*?

The Bible gives God many names and titles, but Savior is the most common. It defines God's work: God saves people. God saves people from danger, like David who escaped the threats of Saul. God saves people from their enemies, like the Israelites who fled through a parted Red Sea and avoided slaughter by the Egyptians. God saves people from distress, like the disciples in the boat who were calmed during a storm when Jesus walked on water.

Of course, not everyone gets spared from enemies, threats, and storms. Even Jesus wasn't saved from death on the cross. The worldly examples of salvation illustrate the critical spiritual meaning of the word *salvation*. God saves people from sin.

The word for salvation in the New Testament, the Greek word *soteria,* is also the same word for health. It is a word with physical, mental, and spiritual dimensions. To speak of salvation is to talk about being made whole. When Jesus quoted the Shema, the central prayer of the Torah, he was relaying God's concern for our wholeness: "Hear, O Israel: the Lord our God, the Lord is one; you shall love the Lord your God with all your heart, and with all your soul, and with all your mind, and with all your strength" (Mark 12:29-30). God yearns that we be one with God. Eventually the physical health of every person will give way, but our spiritual health, our oneness with God, does not have to. God ultimately desires to save us from the forces that can rob us of spiritual wholeness.

Most of us hunger for wholeness. Most of us desire a sense of purpose, meaning, and contentment. As Christians, we want to love others, ourselves, and God more completely. We want to live in such a way as to have no gap between ideals and actions.

This is the sense of wholeness the Bible first depicts in the opening story of Adam and Eve. They lived with each other and with God with no fear, separation, or shame. What damaged this condition of wholeness was sin. We will explore the topic of sin more fully in chapter 5, but for now let's simply think of sin as the force that makes us prefer our way to God's way. Sin is less about our actions and more a description of our condition. We feel inclined to seek our own way. As the hymn writer described in "Come, Thou Fount of Every Blessing": "Prone to wander, Lord, I feel it, prone to leave the God I love." We create this separation on our own; this is part of our human condition. But we alone cannot remove the separation. Only God can do that.

The story of the Bible is the stunning drama about God's ongoing action to bridge the distance between us and God. Over and over again, God uses sacrifice as a means to forgive, beginning with Adam and Eve. When they became aware of their nakedness and were ashamed, God sacrificed animals and used their hides to clothe the couple. When the Israelites broke the laws God gave them in the wilderness, once a year God directed them to tie a scarlet ribbon onto the head of a scapegoat representing all the sins of the community and release the animal into the wilderness, symbolizing God's taking away the sins of the people. Eventually, God arrived in person in the form of Jesus, who died on a cross. Christians came to view the cross as a symbol of God's sacrificial love and readiness to forgive and restore a broken humanity.

The story of the Bible is the story of God's willingness to sacrifice for the forgiveness of sin. God could choose to forgive us without making a sacrifice, but where are we without that sacrifice? Deep down we all know that sin costs. Just being told that God loves us and forgives us seems shallow and unconvincing. The actions we commit that come out of brokenness do damage. Sometimes we can pay for the damage. For example, if we break something of value, we may be able to pay for the cost of the repair ourselves. But what happens when the item is irreplaceable? Sometimes our sin damages in ways money can't repair. Words cut deeply. Dignity and self-worth are not easily restored. The cross reminds us that only God can make the payment to restore us to wholeness.

For my daily devotions I read *The One Year Bible*. At the time of this writing, I am slogging through the Old Testament Book of Leviticus. There's nothing like starting your morning with pages of ancient laws and rituals! But a few days ago I read details about what the Israelites were to do after they had wronged someone or offended God. Depending on the infraction, they brought certain types of sacrifices to the tabernacle. They presented their offering to the priest, who burned it on the altar. As the fire consumed the gift and smoke billowed to the sky, it signified the cleansing of their sin.

As I read this, the thought occurred to me that Old Testament people believed they could take action that would bring forgiveness. We know the practice of sacrifice created problems over time. Forgiveness became bound by what people did. What was meant to be an experience of God's mercy—making an offering—became a requirement for earning or meriting God's forgiveness.

Then came the story of Jesus and the cross, and God made it quite clear: Forgiveness is freely given, not earned. The cross represents cost, and grace is not cheap. Only God can pay the price. Jesus' death on the cross is a gift, and salvation comes through this self-sacrifice. Accepting it acknowledges the cost of sin and God's ceaseless effort to redeem and restore us.

There's a story about a wealthy American who ordered a custom Rolls-Royce from England. Not long after he started driving it, he experienced a mechanical problem. He called the company, and a mechanic flew over from England to fix it. Many weeks later, the owner still hadn't received a repair bill, so he called the company to ask about it. The person who answered the phone could find nothing in the records and summoned the manager. A few minutes later, the manager came to the phone, and in a distinct British accent said, "Sir, we have no record of a Rolls-Royce ever having had mechanical failure."

I tell this story because I think of Jesus as the mechanic sent from God to repair us. (Maybe not a stretch in a book with a car-racing theme.) When we accept this gift, then one day God will check the record of our lives. We will expect to hear a review of all the damages we have caused, but God will look up and say, "I have no record of failure for my servant."

Some may ask, If God bears the entire price for our sin, then why doesn't that give us a blank check to sin? Why isn't God's unmerited forgiveness an invitation to do whatever we want, knowing the price has already been paid? And the answer is pretty simple: because breaking down is no fun. We are intended to run the way our Creator designed us.

What Does It Mean to Call Jesus *Lord*?

Now, let's look at the second important word in the apostle Paul's counsel: *Lord.* Keep in mind that in the Bible, the word *lord* was not exclusively religious. It applied to anyone who had power and authority over others, such as "the lord of the manor." It also designated nobility, as Great Britain still does with its House of Lords.

But what is a lord? Let's borrow an analogy from auto racing and see if that helps. Let's consider the crew chief.

This is the person who leads the pit crew, coordinates pit stops, makes sure the car is in tiptop shape, and stays in radio contact with the driver throughout the entire race. Working from an elevated position beside the track, the crew chief actually has a much better view of the race than the driver does. The crew chief anticipates challenges in ways the driver can't. He can see opportunities to shave time off the clock that the driver can't. For instance, Richard Petty won the 1981 Daytona 500 because his crew chief called off a tire change, saving him precious seconds and giving him the edge. Gordon Johncock won the 1982 Indy 500 by 0.16 seconds because his crew chief made the call to give the car just enough gas to get through the race rather than topping off the tank, again saving precious seconds.

Without crew chiefs, drivers would be on their own—and that would create chaotic conditions. Our lives are the same way. We all need a higher authority to direct us, guide us, and help us steer through the challenges of life.

Accepting that we can't go it alone means letting God be God. Sometimes what sounds like faith is actually a veiled attempt to maintain full control. We fervently pray, asking God to do what we want done. This may seem like deep trust on our part, but in reality it is an attempt to use faith to get our way, not God's. When such efforts fail, we grow resentful or miss the larger ways in which God provides answers.

By admitting we need God's help and guidance, we are trusting that God is seeing the bigger picture, just as the crew chief has a better view of the track. Admitting that we aren't in full control means conceding that there are mysteries too big for us to fathom and problems too great for us to understand, much less solve.

I was only sixteen years old when I realized how much I needed a crew chief, someone to direct my life. I remember the power of wanting to be accepted and to fit in. I recall how much I wanted to go it alone, and yet I realized how quickly I could steer myself into a wall. Along the way, through the influence of my church, my pastors, and my mentors, I learned what it meant to have a Lord and Savior. I discovered that Jesus loved me no matter what mistakes I made and that he knew me better than anyone. And one day I took that step and crossed the starting line of faith.

In his book *Running on Empty*, Fil Anderson, former national training director for Young Life, recalls reading an interview with a member of the Boston Philharmonic Orchestra. The interviewer asked the orchestra member how it feels to get a standing ovation after a performance or a negative review the next morning. The musician said she once was greatly affected by audiences and critics, but over time she came to value only the conductor's approval. Now listen to this important sentence in Anderson's book: "Her logic was simple; her conductor was the only person in the crowd who really knew how she was supposed to perform."[1]

Fil Anderson could have just as easily been talking about a crew chief who knows how the car and driver are supposed to perform. This is what Jesus Christ does for us. When we invite Jesus to be our Lord, we aren't asking him to be our boss. We are inviting him to bring out our best. He is the only one who knows how we are supposed to perform.

Whether we intend to or not, we pick up a lot of lords in life. To quote the great theologian Bob Dylan, "You're gonna have to serve somebody."[2] We have people whose opinions of us can greatly affect us. Their words can lift us up or tear us down. But as well-intentioned as some people might be, there is only one Lord who knows everything about us, who understands us completely, who will help us to be our best. This is a conviction we need to embrace over and over again because the other lords will never stop vying for our attention.

It's not enough to accept Jesus Christ as Lord and Savior once and call it good. That asks too much of our human condition. We all need restarts.

The same is true in auto racing. There's never been a race run where the green flag appeared only once. For various reasons, every race has pauses and even full stops many times before the winner crosses the finish line. The green flag comes out again after every pause and every stop to restart the race.

I've found that I often need to take the green flag over and over. I need to return to the basics, the truth that first and foremost God loves me and forgives me, and that God offers God's power to bring out my best.

How about you? The crucial spiritual message about the green flag is that God is a God of fresh starts. That's plural, not singular.

Frequently we need to say, "God, I accept again your forgiveness. I need your direction in my life. I don't want to just coast. I need to be revved up. I need a fresh touch of your mercy. I need your healing. I choose all over again to make the one you sent, Jesus Christ, my Lord and Savior."

Do you feel the roar?

Reflection Questions

1. How would you describe the pace of your spiritual life right now: Full throttle? Reduced speed? Just coasting? Or some other description?

2. How do you respond to the idea that faith is trust and action?

3. What does the phrase "accepting Jesus Christ as Lord and Savior" mean to you?

4. Why do you think sacrifice is associated with forgiveness of sin?

5. How does the idea of Jesus as a crew chief match your relationship with Jesus?

6. How have you experienced a time when you needed to restart your race?

Notes

THE YELLOW FLAG

Heeding the Cautions

Matthew 4:1-11

In the climactic scene of the 1990 movie *Days of Thunder*, hotshot race-car driver Cole Trickle, played by Tom Cruise, is in the final laps of the Daytona 500. He's running near the top of the leaderboard when suddenly there's a crash up ahead. Crew chief Harry Hogge, played by Robert Duvall, radios Trickle to tell him that he can maneuver around the crash and debris only if he stays on the high side of the track. He won't be able to see through the smoke; but if he keeps at full speed, he'll be in position to win.[1]

The camera work, editing, and sound all give you a good sense of what it would be like to drive a race car through blinding smoke. Trickle presses on the gas pedal as the music swells. You feel his fear as he races through the haze and then his relief as he emerges unscathed on the other side. It makes for great drama. It makes for great cinematic tension. And it makes for really bad racing.

What Hollywood portrays as gutsy is, in reality . . . well . . . stupid. It's also never going to happen. In an actual race, the moment a crash occurs, the yellow caution flag is waved. Drivers have to reduce their speed immediately and follow behind the safety car, or "pace car," whose job is to limit speeds until the accident is cleared.

Caution flags increase driver safety by also signaling the potential for an accident. Spotters are strategically located around the track to watch not only for crashes but also for hazardous debris, which is often the result of incidental contact between cars or with the outer walls. Under the caution flag, laps still count toward the full number of laps needed to finish the race. Four to five laps are generally completed per flag; on average, the yellow flag appears eight times in a race.

Racing well means heeding these cautions. The same is true in terms of the spiritual life.

Have you ever had your race of life interrupted by a caution flag of some sort? Have you ever experienced the need to slow your pace because you've gotten some warning signs that danger is imminent? Maybe a doctor has warned you about the potential of a heart attack or some other serious health risk if you don't make lifestyle changes. Maybe your spouse or a family member has asked you tough questions because they're concerned about personality changes in you. Maybe a friend or a colleague has confronted you about drinking or displays of anger or other inappropriate behavior. Maybe you've found yourself thinking about your life and saying to yourself words to this effect: *If things don't change, I don't think I will be able to . . .*

If you have had experiences like these, you might think of them as spiritual yellow flags. Whether God is speaking to us through other people or through direct intervention, God will not let us crash without first giving us cautions. We could say that the closer we get to God, the better we learn to recognize spiritual yellow flags.

One of the first things we observe about Jesus' ministry is how he learned to heed cautions. Actually, Jesus learned this lesson before his ministry even began. Immediately after being baptized by John the Baptist, God's Spirit descended upon Jesus like a dove, and Jesus heard a voice from heaven, saying, "This is my Son, the Beloved, with whom I am well pleased" (Matt. 3:17). That was Jesus' green flag. That was his "start your engine" moment. Yet Jesus' initial laps were under a caution flag: God first sent him into the wilderness to be tested.

After fasting for forty days, Jesus faced his adversary, the devil. This was not a random experience. The devil didn't just appear. God appointed it. Why? Because Jesus needed to recognize the "debris" that could wreck him. Before he hit full speed, Jesus had to be confronted with the potential dangers that could keep him from completing his race.

This is a significant detail in Jesus' life that I want to examine fully in this chapter. God sent Jesus to be tested! And if Jesus had to be tested, what does that mean for you and me?

Since the days of early Christianity, we have come to understand the nature of Jesus as both fully human and fully divine. Yes, he was the son of God, but he also experienced life as completely as you and I do. Part of that experience means realizing that no one—not even Jesus—is immune to the possibility of crashes.

What happens when we ignore the warnings? The story of Centralia, Pennsylvania, offers a blunt answer. It was a small, stable town in the heart of coal-mining country. It may have seemed like a quiet, happy, even predictable place to live. Have you noticed I'm referring to Centralia in the past tense? That's because, for the most part, it no longer exists.

In 1962, a landfill in the town caught on fire. Local firefighters thought they had put out the blaze, but it went underground, spreading into the vast web of coal veins. Soon, residents were seeing smoke seeping from the ground. If swift, aggressive action had been taken early on, the fire could have been extinguished. But every attempt fell short, and the town eventually gave up. In the 1980s, as deadly sinkholes began appearing and people were passing out from the fire's fumes, the federal government finally stepped in to relocate the residents at a cost of millions of dollars. Today, the town has been demolished except for a few homeowners who refused to leave, and Centralia is a grid of ghostly streets. The fire is expected to burn for another two hundred and fifty years.

In metaphorical terms, we might think of Centralia as a picture of the human condition. We all have potential "debris" in our lives that, when ignored or improperly handled, can catch fire and get out of control. Maybe it's an urge we believe we can contain, an attraction we tell ourselves is just platonic, a revenge we fantasize playing out, or an ambition we think is worth any price. As the saying goes, "If you play with fire, you get burned." But most wildfires burn far more people than the ones who start them.

How we deal with our debris—both the real and potential hazards that loom in our lives—is important. God does not want debris to wreck us. Like a spotter at the racetrack, God is always on the lookout for what can cause us problems. Part of the benefit of living a spiritual life and following God's direction is learning to recognize and heed the cautions God sends our way. In the race of life, we all have to do our own driving, but those who finish the race are the ones who have learned to heed heavenly warnings.

What does this look like in practice? What brings out a caution flag in the spiritual life, and how should we respond? Let's take a closer look at the temptations Jesus faced—his caution-flag experiences—and see how we might relate to them.

All three temptations came at the close of his time in the wilderness. The first dealt with food. Jesus had not eaten for forty days, and the devil came to him and said, "If you are the Son of God, command these stones to become loaves of bread." Jesus responded by quoting Deuteronomy: "One does not live by bread alone, but by every word that comes from the mouth of God" (Matt. 4:3-4). Now, let's pause here for a moment. How well can you relate to that temptation? Does it make you think, *This story doesn't apply to me. I don't have the power to turn stones into bread. This kind of temptation is only for someone fully divine.*

But not so fast. Instead of focusing on turning stones into bread, try thinking of this temptation as using whatever power or ability you have to satisfy yourself. That gets a lot closer to our human experience, doesn't it?

I well remember when pro golfer Tiger Woods apologized for his much-publicized infidelities that eventually broke up his marriage. "I convinced myself that normal rules didn't apply," he said during his news conference. "I thought I could get away with whatever I wanted. I felt that I had worked hard my entire life and deserved to enjoy all the temptations around me. I felt I was entitled."[2]

Well, you don't have to be Tiger Woods—or even Jesus, for that matter—to understand what it's like to be tempted to use your ability or stature to satisfy yourself. Perhaps your position makes you susceptible to exploiting people to get what you want. Perhaps your influence with a business acquaintance or a member of the church tempts you to seek special treatment. Or maybe you have learned how to employ intimidation to get certain people to agree with you or accommodate you. Every one of us can fall prey to abusing power, privilege, and trust.

This lesson hit home to me years ago at a church I once served. One of the members who counted our offering began to notice that the amount of paper currency was shrinking from week to week. But he was an older man who at times could get a bit confused, so his concerns were initially dismissed. Finally, the church's financial secretary did some checking and realized the man was right. Contributions in the form of paper bills had significantly dropped over a nine-month period.

We thought we had a secure system: At least two people were with the offering plates at all times. After worship services, the money was put into bags, which were sealed and locked inside a safe. On Mondays, a team of counters broke the seals to open the bags. We couldn't figure out how anyone could get to the money, so we called in the sheriff's department to set up camera surveillance. What we discovered was an employee who had access to the financial secretary's office where the safe's keys and offering bags were kept. On Sunday nights he stole the cash, sealed the remaining money in new offering bags, and returned them to the safe. Over the course of nine months, he had stolen $28,000!

Now, that may sound really sinister, but we also learned the person was going through a rough patch. His family was struggling financially. The first time he took the money, he told himself he would pay it back eventually. Then, as he continued to steal, he convinced himself that he had actually earned the money because of the extra things he did in his job. Later he said, "The first time I did it, I knew it was wrong; but after a while, I stopped thinking about it." He abused the trust the church had placed in him and learned to ignore the twinge of conscience. He had driven through the caution flag without slowing down.

Can you relate a little better now to the temptation to turn stones into bread?

Let's consider the next caution flag Jesus experienced. The Bible says that the devil then took Jesus to the pinnacle of the temple and dared him to jump. In the "RSV" translation (Rob's Standard Version), I can imagine the devil arguing, "Doesn't the Bible say God will not let anything happen to holy ones? Won't God send angels to catch them?" Once more, Jesus quoted Deuteronomy as a response to the devil: "Do not put the Lord your God to the test" (Matt. 4:5-7).

Again, it may be easy to write off this kind of temptation. Who could be coaxed into jumping off a building to test God?

But once again, I'll ask you to consider this temptation a little differently. Think of it as putting yourself in a potentially dangerous place while still believing you will be spared any consequences. Like getting behind the wheel of a car after too many drinks, convinced you'll be fine. Or letting a friend talk you into doing something wrong for fear you'll appear weak if you don't. Or spending intimate time alone with someone you're attracted to when you're already in a committed relationship.

When we're focused on how close we can creep to the edge, we can fool ourselves into thinking we won't fall. But as we near the precipice, God is there to wave a caution flag. In that moment we have a choice to make: Heed the flag and do what it takes to get to safety or ignore the caution and hope for the best.

When my wife, Susan, was a church youth director, a boy in her group got into a car with several friends one night. He later acknowledged that even as he climbed in, he had a strong feeling that he shouldn't. The other youths ended up committing a crime that evening. Though this particular boy didn't join in the wrongdoing, he was convicted as an accessory.

Not heeding a caution can drastically change life in an instant. The advice of scripture, upon which Jesus relies, is always to take the approach of "do not put the Lord to the test." As James advises, "Submit yourselves therefore to God. Resist the devil, and he will flee from you" (4:7).

In the third and final temptation, the devil showed Jesus all the kingdoms of the world and said, "All these I will give you, if you will fall down and worship me." Once again, Jesus rebuked the devil by relying on God's word in Deuteronomy: "Worship the Lord your God, and serve only him" (Matt. 4:9-10). This is the temptation that I think was the most dangerous for Jesus. What more could he want than for everyone in the world to be under his authority? After all, Jesus came "so that at the name of Jesus every knee should bend, . . . and every tongue should confess that Jesus Christ is Lord" (Phil. 2:10-11).

Surely this time we can safely say this temptation doesn't apply to us. No one can relate to being offered authority over all the kingdoms of the world, right?

But can you relate to the desire to take a shortcut to your goals? Jesus was being tempted to reach his goal by bypassing the cross. That had to be an enticing offer. Why would he want to face crucifixion if he could take another path to world dominion? But there's the deception: The destination would not be the same. Jesus wasn't sent to create some kind of heavy-handed dictatorship. Rather, Jesus' way of life is the way of forgiveness, compassion, and self-surrender.

Without the cross—without Jesus giving his own life to save ours (John 10:11)—the ultimate object of worship would not be the self-sacrificing, unconditionally loving God. Shortcuts that avoid necessary challenges do not take us where we really want to go.

Does this temptation become more understandable to you? Your goals may be noble, but that doesn't mean any path will get you there. The path you choose is as important as where the path takes you. A lot of good people hit debris while pursuing worthwhile things.

I know of a pastor who learned this lesson the hard way. A few years ago, he was serving a fast-growing church in the Midwest. The congregation needed a new sanctuary, but they were unable to secure a loan for the needed amount. The pastor grew impatient. People were flocking to the church. He couldn't wait. So he falsified bank documents to take out a personal loan. It was all for a great cause, right? Of course the truth came out, and the pastor had to resign. Eventually, the church closed its doors.

Speed and debris do not go together. Avoiding the debris requires slowing down. Caution flags may lengthen the time of a race, but remember, the laps still count! There are no shortcuts.

So, this Gospel story is not only about Jesus' temptations. It's also about our temptations. Like Jesus, we can be tempted to take shortcuts, to put ourselves in dangerous positions, to use our power to satisfy ourselves. The debris that could have caused problems in Jesus' life can cause problems in ours as well.

But before we leave this story behind, let's consider a few more lessons we can take away. First, because Jesus overcame his temptations, he can help us overcome ours. Hebrews 2:18 says, "Because [Jesus] himself was tested by what he suffered, he is able to help those who are being tested."

When Jesus was tempted, he quoted scripture. But I don't believe simply repeating a Bible passage is what makes us immune to temptations. Jesus actually redirected his focus to his God-given mission. Do you ever find that surrendering to temptation is easiest when you feel weary, defeated, or overwhelmed? When I get to that place, I know I stop thinking about the consequences. That's exactly when I need to redirect my focus.

Race-car drivers do this once the caution flag is waved: Their focus shifts from trying to win the race to following the pace car. The pace car sets the appropriate speed for the track's conditions and makes sure the drivers steer safely around the debris.

We can develop our own disciplines to help us set our focus on Jesus as he guides us through temptation. These can include worship, prayer, scripture reading, and fasting. One simple habit I practice is inspired by a 1945 painting, titled *Divine Counselor*, by American illustrator Harry Anderson. It pictures Jesus seated across from a businessman at his desk. The man listens as Jesus talks to him. The picture makes you wonder, *What are they talking about? What did the man ask Jesus? What's he saying that has the man listening so intently?* It makes me want to seek just such a relationship with the Divine Counselor. Sometime you might try what I do: Imagine Jesus sitting in an empty chair beside you. Ask him the questions that are challenging you. Tell him what is on your heart. Then be still. You may be surprised by the responses you get.

Another lesson to take away from Jesus' time in the wilderness is that temptation is a sign of God's presence, not God's absence. Remember that the caution flags waved at Jesus signaled that God was still leading him. When we struggle with temptation, we may think something is wrong with us. We may even think that if we were better people, we wouldn't have these struggles. Or we might wonder why God isn't helping us more. But such experiences reveal not what's wrong with us, but what's right with us. The closer we get to God, the more we become aware of all that is not godly.

Renowned twentieth-century preacher Harry Emerson Fosdick once preached a sermon titled "Preventive Religion." He based it on this verse from Jude: "Now to him who is able to keep you from falling" (v. 24). Fosdick makes the point that while God is in the business of rescue and recovery work, God is even more concerned with keeping us from needing it.[3]

That is why the writer of Hebrews said, "We have a [high priest] who in every respect has been tested as we are, yet without sin. Let us therefore approach the throne of grace with boldness, so that we may receive mercy and find grace to help in time of need" (4:15-16).

Through our relationship with Jesus, God does not leave us to get through the trials alone.

How can we more fully experience this reality? One essential way is to connect to a spiritual community. In a small group of trusted relationships, Christ's presence and power is experienced in a way I'm not sure can be found anywhere else. Knowing that you don't have to bear your struggles quietly can feel lifesaving. Knowing that others also struggle can feel life-affirming.

As a United Methodist, I frequently have to remind myself that this is how our church began. A group of Christians asked John Wesley, an evangelical Anglican pastor, to meet with them to "flee from the wrath to come" (Matt. 3:7). That was eighteenth-century speak for "help us to heed spiritual cautions." They began meeting, and the unique experiences of God that people discovered in this group began to spread, first across London, then throughout England, then across Europe and America. As people honestly reflected on the caution flags in their lives and as they sought God's help together, they found grace when they needed it most.

Think about it. A whole denomination started with a small group of people who were driving under the yellow flag of caution.

Reflection Questions

1. How do you finish the sentence, "If things don't change in my life, I don't think I'll be able to . . ."?
2. What do you make of the idea that God sent Jesus into the wilderness to be tempted?
3. When have you put yourself in a risky position in the belief that nothing bad would happen to you?
4. When have you been tempted to break rules or take a shortcut to achieve success?
5. How do you think guilt can be a sign of our closeness to God rather than our distance from God?

Notes

⫸⫸⫸ 3

THE BLUE FLAG

Moving to
the Outside Lane

Matthew 20:29-34

As a three-time winner of the Indianapolis 500, Hélio Castroneves has probably never had a blue flag waved at him in a race. This flag means you are about to be lapped, and it tells you to move to the outside lane to make way for the car that's a full revolution ahead of you. Hélio jokingly says a blue flag "means someone else is having a better day than you."

Heeding the blue flag isn't mandatory. There is no penalty for ignoring it. That's why it's also called "the courtesy flag." You obey it, Hélio says, because "it's the right thing to do." That's his philosophy both on and off the track: Many of the important things we do in life are done not because we have to do them. We do them because they are right. "Being humble," Hélio says, "takes you far."

For a sport that is all about being faster than your opponents, humility wouldn't seem to be a characteristic of winners. As Will Ferrell's Ricky Bobby says in the movie *Talladega Nights*, "If you ain't first, you're last."[1] Yet even in racing there comes a time when the right thing to do is to turn your attention to someone else's race.

Author Stephen R. Covey offers a picture of what this looks like in his best-selling book *The 7 Habits of Highly Effective People*. He tells the story of riding the New York subway one weekend morning when a father with small children entered the car. The scene had been quiet, with people reading or resting their eyes. But the children changed all that, running around, yelling, and throwing things. The father sat with his eyes closed, seemingly oblivious to the commotion. Covey writes that it was hard not to feel irritated. This man's children were being disruptive, and he was being insensitive to other riders by not disciplining them.

Finally, Covey said to the man, "Sir, your children are really disturbing a lot of people. I wonder if you couldn't control them more?" The man opened his eyes as if just realizing what was happening. He said, "Oh, you're right. I guess I should do something about it. We just came from the hospital, where their mother died about an hour ago. I don't know what to think, and I guess they don't know how to handle it either." Suddenly Covey's focus shifted. The situation wasn't about his own race anymore. It was about someone else's and what he could do for that person. Stephen Covey was invited to let go of his moment of irritation and see what he could do to help someone in need.[2]

That is what you can call a blue-flag moment. God is making you aware of an opportunity to set aside your own concerns and interests and to focus on another person's needs. People who receive a blue flag recognize that they are in a circumstance where they can help someone else. They have a chance to do the right thing. A major part of the spiritual life involves taking the blue flag. But just like in racing, responding to this signal in life isn't mandatory, and it can be easily ignored.

Spiritual blue flags may be waved at us in any number of ways. You may notice, for example, that a colleague looks distraught as you are leaving the office for the day. You ask whether the person needs anything, and you get the response, "No, I don't want to bother you." You can keep heading to your car . . . or you can decide to heed the blue flag.

Or you may be trying to get to your airport gate, but you over-hear an elderly couple speaking a foreign language, and they appear confused. You realize they are probably having trouble understanding a sign. You think about stopping to help, but you know it will delay you. You can keep walking to your gate . . . or you can decide to heed the blue flag.

Or you may be sitting in church on a beautiful, sunny day, and all you're able to think about is your tee time that afternoon. Then the pastor snaps you out of your daydream with a request for volunteers to teach children's Sunday school. Normally such requests go right past you, but this time you leave church bothered because you feel a tug to respond. You can go on with your day . . . or you can decide to heed the blue flag.

No one can anticipate when blue flags will be waved, and they often show up when it's inconvenient. It's easy to feel resentful or frustrated at being the one who is getting the signals, but learning to heed them can take us far in life.

Jesus demonstrated a blue-flag way of life for his followers. Paul would later write to the Philippians that moving over for others is the very reason that Jesus came to earth: "Let the same mind be in you that was in Christ Jesus, who, though he was in the form of God, did not regard equality with God as something to be exploited, but emptied himself, taking the form of a slave, being born in human likeness" (Phil. 5:2-7).

Jesus demonstrated this "giving up privileges" attitude as much as he preached it. He took time to bless children when others tried to persuade him he had more pressing business. He washed the feet of the disciples in the upper room. He regularly responded to people needing his help, such as a synagogue leader whose daughter had died, a Roman centurion whose servant was sick, and nameless crowds with endless infirmities. But perhaps the best illustration of Jesus' willingness to move aside for others happened one day in Jericho.

Jesus and his disciples had just been in Judea, on the eastern side of the Jordan River. They were beginning their ascent to Jerusalem. As they passed through Jericho, a large crowd surrounded Jesus. Two blind men sat by the road, and when they learned Jesus was approaching, they started shouting, "Lord, have mercy on us, Son of David!" The crowd tried to quiet the men, but they shouted louder. Jesus asked them, "What do you want me to do for you?" They answered, "Lord, let our eyes be opened." Jesus touched their eyes and healed them, and the men rose and followed Jesus. (See Matthew 20:29-34.)

Macroanalysis and Microanalysis

To appreciate why this story is such a good example of Jesus' blue-flag way of life, we need to zoom out for a moment and consider the larger sequence and setting of the story, and then zoom back in to review some details. Zooming out we can see that this was the last event in the Gospel of Matthew before Jesus triumphantly entered Jerusalem on what we call Palm Sunday. What started in celebration on Palm Sunday ended a few days later with Jesus' arrest, trial, and crucifixion. On the way to Jericho, Jesus had warned the disciples that these things would occur once they reached Jerusalem. He prepared them for the cross.

Yet the very next episode in the chapter (Matt. 20:20-28) tells about the mother of disciples James and John asking Jesus to grant her sons positions of honor in his kingdom. This ignited a division within the fellowship of Jesus' most loyal followers. Jesus quickly dealt with the situation and called them together. In the "RSV" translation (again, Rob's Standard Version), I imagine both sternness and disappointment in his voice: "What the heck are you doing? Worrying about a pecking order is what people expect from the rest of the world. You are supposed to be different! If you want to be great, then act like a servant. Act like me, for goodness' sake! That's why I came, to move aside for others!" (See Matthew 20:20-28.)

Now let's zoom in on the next verses, which describe Jesus and the disciples visiting Jericho. As they were leaving the town, crowds packed around Jesus. Don't you wonder what kind of people they were? Perhaps there were folks who sought healing or help of some kind—in other words, needy people. Perhaps there were people who knew where Jesus was headed and who were curious whether he was the Messiah they were anticipating, a military king who would overthrow the Roman rule. Perhaps they were just observers who believed they could see something interesting if they stayed close to Jesus. I imagine the crowd being all of the above: people who, for different reasons, had their own expectations of Jesus. Therefore, it makes sense when the crowd rebuked a couple of blind men trying to get Jesus' attention. To them, these "losers" were nothing more than a distraction, an interruption to what they wanted from Jesus.

There also seems to be something about how the two men addressed Jesus that got his attention. They shouted, "Son of David." While this phrase appears several times in the Gospels, it is not one of the more popular designations for Jesus, and it is not one Jesus ever used for himself. It was a distinctly messianic title. Perhaps the two men thought that shouting the most revered title they knew would catch Jesus' ear. They probably were desperate enough to do whatever they could to get Jesus' attention; maybe they thought he was their best chance to regain their sight.

Jesus could easily have been consumed with his own "race," his own mission and ultimate purpose. He was surrounded by people who obviously felt their needs were more pressing than those of a couple of blind men. Yet Jesus stopped and went to their aid.

His example points us to lessons we can learn about spiritual blue flags and the importance of moving to the outside lane to make way for others. Here are four questions to guide us.

Who Has Moved Over for Me?

First, try relating to the blind men. What would it be like to have been in their place? How would you have felt in that culture if you had to depend on begging from others to survive? Imagine being treated as if your needs didn't matter. Remember that the people of this era tended to believe bad things happened to you as the result of bad choices you made and that suffering was the result of God's punishment. What would that way of thinking do to your own faith over time? Have you ever been in a place where you were totally dependent on someone to take notice of your situation and help you? "Moving to the outside lane," slowing down your pace and taking your focus off yourself to help someone else, begins with recognizing that others have done the same for us.

My friend Charles Harrison is the senior pastor of Barnes United Methodist Church in downtown Indianapolis. He also started the city's Ten Point Coalition, an organization that serves at-risk youth and seeks to reduce violence in the city. He and other volunteers walk the meanest streets of Indianapolis on Friday and Saturday nights to be a presence of peace. They get to know kids and families. They are all about "moving aside" for the sake of our city.

What motivates Charles? When he was fourteen years old and growing up in Louisville, Kentucky, his brother was shot and killed. Charles was so enraged that he decided he was going to kill the person responsible. Men in his church found out what he was planning and had a "come to Jesus" meeting with him. They told Charles they were not going to let him go through with his plan. They listened as he poured out his anger and grief, and they reassured him he would not be alone in facing his pain. Charles knows without a doubt that had it not been for that intervention, he wouldn't be here today.

You might not have had an experience quite so dramatic, but do you have people in your life to whom you can say, "I wouldn't be here today if not for them"? What names would be on your list?

One name on mine is Mildred Swicegood. Her husband was a Presbyterian pastor. Their son went to Pfeiffer College (now Pfeiffer University), a United Methodist school in Misenheimer, North Carolina. When Mildred's husband passed away in 1975, she took a sizable portion of the estate she received and established an endowed scholarship to help students going into full-time Christian service. I was a recipient of that scholarship, and while I attended Pfeiffer, my dad learned that Mildred lived just a few blocks from our family home in Winston-Salem.

Once when I was on a school break, I decided to visit Mildred and thank her for this scholarship that was providing a significant portion of my tuition. I expected to drive up to an estate. After all, you have to be extraordinarily rich to endow a scholarship like that, right? I was surprised to pull up to a modest two-bedroom condominium. Mildred invited me inside. She was grateful for my visit, and she told me about her husband and their desire to help future ministers with their education. Although their son didn't go into ministry, they had been impressed with Pfeiffer, so that was where she chose to place her investment. I left Mildred's home that day thinking of all the things she could have done with the money. She could have taken luxury cruises, purchased a mansion, or practiced retail therapy every day. Instead, she wanted to help students like me. I think of her often, and I ask God to help me carry out my ministry in a way that is worthy of her sacrifice.

What Is Winning All About?

Moving to the outside lane to make way for others also redefines what winning is. Do we think of winning in terms of where we end up or in terms of what happens along the way? That is a crucial question. If winning is the former, then we'll seldom have time to be interrupted by blue flags; winning will clearly be determined by whether we reach our own goal. However, if winning means the latter, then the goal is not just about where we finish but also *how* we race.

Author and pastor Herb Miller once told a story about a horse race where the two leaders were involved in a terrible collision just yards from the finish line. Horses and riders went tumbling across the track. The jockey quickest to his feet hastily grabbed the reins, pulled the horse up, jumped on, and finished the race first, only to learn that he had lost: He had mounted the wrong horse! *How* he finished was as important as where he finished.

Many people in life reach amazing goals, only to discover they were riding the wrong horse. Think of the litany of contemporary "winners" who have brought disgrace on themselves: Bernie Madoff, Kenneth Lay, John Edwards, and Lance Armstrong, just to name a few. Winning isn't everything when it's the only thing.

Jesus was on his way to Jerusalem. He was walking to his death. Under the circumstances you wouldn't blame him for not stopping to help a couple of blind men, but he did. He stopped because helping others was the true mark of what it meant to cross the finish line in the race of life. We will examine this topic more thoroughly in chapters 6 and 7, but as a way to prepare, try this exercise now. In one sentence, write your personal definition of winning. Then write down what you hope people will say about you at your funeral. How well do your two answers intersect? Chances are the intersections will have something to do with how well you heed blue-flag moments along the way.

How Can I Make an Impact on People?

The story in Matthew 20 says that Jesus touched the two blind men, and they received their sight. Don't get too caught up in the miraculous nature of Jesus' touch. The point is that he did for these men what was in his power to do at that moment.

What is in your power to do for others? Are you in a position financially to help alleviate suffering? Do you have skills to teach and mentor children or young adults? Are you good with your hands in a way that you can offer practical assistance to people? Instead of focusing solely on others' needs, focus on the gifts you have to offer. We can easily convince ourselves that because we can't give people everything they need, we don't have anything to offer. But when we start with what we have and vow to use it to serve faithfully, there is no telling what God can do. Here is a truth about you and me: Each of us has the power to make a difference in others' lives. No matter what we have, God can use us to touch people.

Barbara Glanz is a business consultant and motivational speaker who tells about being hired by a supermarket chain to lead a workshop on customer service. She challenged the employees to think of ways they could make a difference in customers' lives and motivate them to return to the store. One seminar participant was a grocery bagger with Down syndrome named Johnny who became captivated by this idea. He noticed how many customers in his checkout line were frowning, so he got the idea to share uplifting quotes every day to brighten people's lives. His dad helped him print out the quotes each night, and Johnny cut the pages into strips and signed his name on the back. He put a strip in a bag for each customer, with a different quote every day.

About a month later, the manager of Johnny's store called Glanz to tell her the impact her seminar had made. He had recently noticed that people were standing three times longer in one checkout line than in the others. The manager tried to direct the customers to shorter lines, but they declined. That's when he realized they were all willing to wait because it was Johnny's line. They wanted to experience his daily touch.[3]

What if we ask God every day, "Lord, what can I do to touch someone? What can I do to make an impact on other people in their race through life?"

How Can I Help Others Get into the Race?

Notice what happened at the end of the episode in Jericho. Once the two men had regained their sight, they followed Jesus. What do you think happened to those two men then? I can see them coming under the influence of Jesus' blue-flag way of life, remembering how he moved aside for them and looking for ways they could touch and help other people. There's no telling how many more people were touched because one blue flag was heeded in Jericho.

Ultimately, heeding God's blue flags brings other people into the race, and it helps others get to the finish line. This may, in fact, be the best way to get people started in a spiritual race. Rather than convincing arguments or flashy resources, what most influences people to become followers of Christ are the Christ-followers who are willing to move aside for others they don't even know.

The church I serve made a bold, risky decision to turn our traditional 11 AM Sunday service into a contemporary worship service. We had three identical Sunday services already; although the best-attended one was at 9:30 AM, more than five hundred people regularly came to the 11 o'clock service. When the change was announced, the vast majority of the 11 o'clock worshipers agreed either to adjust to the new style or to make a change in their Sunday routine and attend one of the earlier services. This was perhaps the most daring display of moving aside I have witnessed in a congregation.

One of the first families to begin attending the new contemporary service was a United Methodist minister who serves in a position outside the local church; his wife, whose father had been a Methodist pastor; and their teenage son. They had been looking for a church home for some time. Their son had been born with many health complications, endured many surgeries, and was considered a medical miracle.

When this family started coming to St. Luke's, the son was not that interested in church. One popular perception, confirmed often for him by his own experience, was that churches are full of hypocrites and people who judge others. For some time, the young man often brought a book with him to read during the service; yet during the first year of the new contemporary service, he became more and more engaged in worship.

In the season of Lent, his family joined a small group in the church dedicated to performing an act of community service during the season. This group decided to help put on an Easter egg hunt at a government-subsidized apartment complex. The son provided the prizes: cherished stuffed animals that he had collected over the years. This was a huge sacrifice. He was willing to lay aside some of his most prized possessions.

The Easter egg hunt was so moving to him that he wrote about it for his school paper. He described the day, the toys he had donated, and the experiences he'd had with the children who received them. He ended with these words:

> I feel like I made a difference in the lives of these kids, and I feel good about it. I was glad to be involved, and the experience has made me remember that even though Christianity has sometimes done bad things throughout history, it does more good than bad. It made me realize that for all the evil in the world, good people can help to ease the pain of others and to make the world a better place.
>
> After we got home, I told my mom, "Of all of the things you've taken me to at church, I liked doing this the best." I remember an old phrase that I try to live by: "If you do good for others, they will do good in return." What that means is, if I do good things for these people, they may do good things for others or for you in the future.

Like the blind men who became followers of Jesus that day in Jericho, this young man joined the spiritual blue-flag effort as a result of a new worship service started by a whole community that moved aside. It sounds so simple, but for all the doom-and-gloom reports about declining church attendance and skepticism about the church's relevance, maybe we just need to heed blue flags.

What can you do to move over for people you don't even know but who might decide to join the race because of your sacrifice?

Reflection Questions

1. In the last twenty-four hours, how many blue-flag opportunities can you recall? Which ones did you respond to? Which did you let go by?

2. What do you think Paul meant in his letter to the Philippians when he urged, "Let the same mind be in you that was in Christ Jesus"?

3. In the story of the two blind men in Jericho, what do you think was on Jesus' mind as he walked through the town? What do you think the crowd that followed Jesus wanted?

4. What times can you recall when people have moved over for you?

5. If you didn't answer the question earlier, what is your one-sentence definition of winning?

6. What acts have people taken that modeled Christlike love and made an impact on your life and faith?

7. How can you become more attuned to blue-flag opportunities in your life?

Notes

>>> 4

THE RED FLAG

The Importance
of the Delay

Luke 5:12-16

A NASCAR driver friend and I were talking one day about the tracks that drivers love the most, and he named several. What, I asked, made them so popular?

"Those are the tracks," he said, "where you can reach the highest speeds."

Of course. Every driver wants to go fast. What a thrill that kind of speed must be! But for driver Conor Daly, going fast is more than just a thrill. A young Christian still in the early years of his career, Conor told me that he feels closest to God when he's going over two hundred miles per hour. If that wouldn't get you praying, I don't know what would!

Conor, who's the son of former Formula One and Champ Car series driver Derek Daly, also told me that what drivers love the least is the red flag. Of course that makes sense, too. A red flag in racing means the same as a red light on the street: STOP. Red flags appear because of circumstances beyond anyone's control, most often rainy weather. That is why the red flag is also known as the delay flag. Its appearance means cars must leave the track and cease all activity. Not even the pit crews can work during a red flag. You can't try to get an advantage during this time. All you can do is wait.

Some drivers, Conor told me, don't handle red flags in a race very well. Understandably, they lose their focus and get frustrated when they have to stop.

Thinking about this, I could immediately see parallels outside the racing world. We place so much value on productivity and being active that we tend to think of any delay as unwanted and avoidable. If we are being still, then we aren't accomplishing anything. Most people like to go fast.

We live in a fast world. I constantly receive advertisements from communications companies claiming that they provide the fastest Internet service. Mobile-phone businesses battle over who has the speediest technology. 4G is better than 3G, right? We demand our mail-order purchases arrive overnight, visit our doctors at "urgent care" centers, and want delivery food "freaky fast."

But this chapter isn't another plea to slow down and smell the roses. After all, a race is not won by taking your time. In a real race, going slow is not an option. And yet another fact is clear: Many drivers say that how they respond to an interruption can actually determine the outcome of a race. The same can be said when our lives come to a halt.

Sooner or later, we all experience circumstances beyond our control that disrupt our "race." We get laid off from our job. A child contracts a life-threatening illness. A storm or fire destroys our home. As I've been writing this chapter, my wife, Susan, got a call from her brother saying their elderly mother is scheduled to have serious surgery in a week. Susan had been racing to get a lot done in the next few weeks. Her calendar was filled with events she was going to attend and projects she planned to complete. But now, all of that has been replaced with crushing uncertainty.

We can't control these events anymore than a driver can make the rain stop. We wonder: *Why do these disruptions have to happen? How will we possibly get through them? How long will it take?* The Bible never answers those questions in a fully satisfying way, but it does say we are not the first to ask them. Just consider the longest red flag in history.

The book of Exodus tells the story of the Israelites, who were slaves in Egypt for four hundred years. That's about the amount of time between present day and when the Mayflower landed. Talk about a delay! During their enslavement, the Israelites prayed two simple prayers: Why? and How long? Eventually God responded by sending a reluctant deliverer named Moses. He prevailed against Pharaoh, ruler of Egypt, and set God's people free. But before you break out the peanuts and party favors, understand that the Israelites would then spend another forty years roaming the wilderness of Sinai before arriving in the Promised Land.

As if four centuries weren't enough, God tacked on another ten percent. What was the purpose?

I like the way John Ortberg addresses this question in his book *If You Want to Walk on Water, You've Got to Get Out of the Boat.* He cites many of the people in the Bible who were stuck in painful uncertainty, including Moses and the Israelites.

"Why?" asks Ortberg, "Why does God make us wait? If he can do anything, why doesn't he bring us relief and help and answers *now*?" Then he offers this gem: "What God does in us while we wait is as important as what it is we are waiting for."[1]

Are you going through any circumstances beyond your control? Are you facing something that has disrupted your race, and you're stuck waiting it out? Read Ortberg's words again: *What God does in us while we wait is as important as what it is we are waiting for.* Let that sink in, then let me tell you about how one man responded to a red flag and improved the quality of his race.

Jim Cotterill was a hard-driving business consultant with a bright future. He often took time away from his family to spend it at work, but he convinced himself that the pace of his life was the price of success. After all, he was doing it for his family! (Can you hear the backfire?)

On a rare family vacation at a lake in Michigan, Jim and his son went for a bicycle ride at sundown. Though it was getting dark, they headed down the uneven path toward the pier. On the ride, Jim felt the ground under his tires turn smoother than usual. The next thing he remembered was staring at a surgical light in the hospital.

He tried to move, but he felt the restraint of tubes down his throat and IV lines in his arm. He would discover that he had been in the hospital for four days. His bike had slipped over an embankment, and he had fallen fifteen feet in a headfirst dive onto large rocks. His back was broken, and doctors doubted he would walk again.

For the next eight months, Jim undertook agonizing physical therapy to try to get his life back. During that time, though, God stirred him in ways that pushed him toward a whole new life. He was moved by the medical team that was serving him, and he was struck by the idea that life is really about service. He felt a new resolve to serve his family and give back to others.

Jim could have chosen several ways to respond to this time "off the track." Remember a lot of race-car drivers choose to just sit and stew when they get the red flag. Instead, Jim chose to wait actively, with a sense of focus and purpose. He opened himself up to listen for God to give him new direction.

I mentioned before that drivers aren't allowed to have their crews work on their cars under a red flag, but it's worth noting here what drivers are allowed to do: They can take food and drink. They can consult with their crew chief to talk about new race strategies. In much the same way, Jim was nourishing himself. He was allowing God to help him form a new life plan. He was finding new purpose by taking the red flag.

Miraculously, Jim experienced a full recovery. He got his body back but not his life—at least not the life he had before. Generosity became the defining characteristic of his new race. Today he runs a successful foundation, helping people use their resources to make a God-given difference for others. He also has made spending time with his family a priority like he never did before. *Sometimes what happens in us while we wait is more important than what it is we are waiting for.*

That was the significance of the Israelites' wanderings in the wilderness. They had forty more years to wait, but the time was not wasted. They developed practices of worship and faithful living. They actively waited. When their red flag finally lifted, they entered the Promised Land as a new generation of people who trusted in God.

Circumstances may stop the race; but with the red flag, God beckons us to find value in the waiting—by using the time to move closer to God, to listen to God for comfort, encouragement, and new direction.

At the same time, make no mistake: God doesn't hold out for rain to try to get our attention. God isn't just a "foul weather" God. Whether or not we're in crisis, God wants us to find value in pausing.

The most obvious proof of that is the practice of keeping the sabbath. The word *sabbath* literally means the same thing as racing's red flag: *to cease*. God wove sabbath rest into the order of life. It is intended to be a day we stop normal productivity so that we can tend to the sacred in our lives. Our world seems in need of reclaiming this practice. Twenty years ago, people who identified themselves as active churchgoers attended on average three Sundays a month. Today that number is down to 1.7—nearly half! Reasons for this vary. More people work on Sundays because of the increased demand for businesses to stay open seven days a week. Sporting events for kids make it increasingly difficult for families to be in church on a weekly basis. My point is not to heap guilt on us. I simply ask whether we get further in life by never stopping.

In her book *Keeping the Sabbath Wholly*, Marva Dawn tells the story of a wagon train heading west in the days of the Oregon Trail. The settlers were devout Christians, so they stopped each week to keep the sabbath. But as winter neared, some in the group became concerned about making it through the rugged terrain in the cold and snow. They argued that they no longer had the luxury of stopping one day out of the week. The dispute was finally resolved by splitting the train into two groups: one that observed the sabbath and the other that didn't. As it turns out, the group that traveled six out of seven days arrived in Oregon first. By resting themselves and their livestock, they made better time.[2] We actually can go farther when we recognize the value of stopping.

I began this chapter with a discussion of forced stops—when unforeseen circumstances take us off track. But it would be hard to write any book about car-racing without addressing the pit stop, the planned pause for refueling, tire changes, and quick tune-ups. It's a tried-and-true maxim that races are won and lost in the pits.

So let's expand our discussion here. Though not true red-flag moments, pits stops are still as necessary to racing as forced stops. Just as drivers can't possibly drive an entire race on one tank of gas and a single set of tires, we can't be expected to run our own race without moments when we intentionally pull off the track.

The sabbath is one type of intentional stop that encourages us to actively wait. Prayer is another.

The story in the Gospel of Luke (5:12-16) illustrates the priority Jesus placed on prayer. Early in his ministry, we see the pace of his life picking up. He heals a man with leprosy, and news of the miracle spreads, causing crowds to seek his attention. You can feel the press of their demands on him. How could Jesus possibly take time for himself when there were so many people in need?

Can you relate to that pressure? Perhaps you've found yourself saying, "I can't stop now with so many things going on." Or "when my work slows down, I'll take more time for myself and family." Or "I don't want to be this busy, but I don't have any choice."

How did Jesus endure the stress? We learn the secret of his success with these words: "Jesus often withdrew to lonely places and prayed" (Luke 5:16). Thinking of it in racing terms, Jesus viewed these pit stops not as a luxury but as a necessity. With his energy depleted, Jesus set aside times to pause, be still, and reconnect with his relationship with God.

"Jesus went to a lonely place to pray . . . ," Henri Nouwen writes in his book *Out of Solitude*, "to grow in the awareness that all the power he had was given to him; . . . that all the works he did were not really his, but the works of the One who had sent him."[3]

Nearly every time the Gospels mention Jesus going away to pray alone, we read that he had just been surrounded by crowds. The greater the demands Jesus faced, the more he needed solitude.

Can you imagine the clamor and interruptions that Jesus must have endured as the center of attention? We know people were literally pulling on his clothes. Do you feel pulled in different directions by today's distractions? Just as we get to the point where we can hear God speaking, our attention can be whisked away with one buzz of a text message. Our minds can quickly drift to a deadline, an appointment, or an obligation—unless we have the concentration and quiet that solitude can bring.

One pastor in the church I serve, Dr. Marion Miller, keeps a chair in an upstairs closet in her home that serves as her solitary place of prayer. She goes there every morning to find a cozy spot and escape distractions. Often she feels God working on her, reminding her of God's grace, refueling her to face the demands of ministry. Other people may lay a mat or a pillow in a corner of a room. Having a devoted space for spending time in the presence of God is important. Over time, it automatically puts us in a "God-focus" when we go there. We enter that space, opening ourselves to God in intentional ways.

Along with sabbath-keeping and prayer, scripture reading offers another intentional stop that helps us center our thoughts and listen to God. As I mentioned in chapter 1, I have used *The One Year Bible* first thing in the morning for the past several years. This devotional Bible divides scripture into daily units from the Old Testament, the New Testament, Psalms, and Proverbs so it takes you through the entire Bible in a year. It provides a prepared set of Bible readings each day, and I'm not left to figure out which passages to study. I then spend quiet time reflecting on what I have read and what individual part or parts of the scripture really speak to me. I'll ask God, "What do you want to say to me through those words?"

Sometimes, not much comes in the way of an answer. More often than not, though, I'll receive a reminder of God's promises or sense what God would have me do about a particular issue. I may receive guidance about a habit I need to change or come to realize painful admissions I need to make. Over the years, I've learned to take the time to write down important ideas and thoughts that may come to me; I've found that if I wait until after I've showered and dressed, I can't recall what those great ideas were!

All these contemplative practices can help us actively wait so that when we are back on the track we actually run better. I've already talked about how they can connect us to God so that we can find guidance, nourishment, comfort, calm. But whether we take an intentional stop or are forced off by unforeseen circumstances, these practices offer us more than a connection to God. They also remind us whom we are racing for.

Have you noticed that race-car drivers have patches with corporate logos all over their suits and cars? Why is that? It's because without sponsors, a racing team can't compete. A sponsor provides the support required to fund a car. Sponsorship can cost as much as thirty-five million dollars! Without that support, a driver and team can't race.

In a similar way, the Bible says that we each wear the logo of a sponsor. We are made in the image of God; the theological term is *imago dei*. We have a sponsor who supports us and provides our value. Racing for this sponsor means our true worth does not depend on outracing others or on collecting whatever earthly trophies might serve as impostors for success.

Maintaining spiritual practices also helps us discover that we receive some blessings only when we stop. John Easterlin is an internationally renowned opera singer who visited our church and participated in worship. I got a chance to sit down with him and hear about several of his experiences while traveling in Europe.

Preparing for a trip that would include sixteen auditions in seven countries over twenty-three days, Easterlin told his sister about his fear of getting lost. She reminded him of what has become a key verse for his life: "The LORD thy God is with thee whithersoever thou goest" (Joshua 1:9, KJV).

On the first leg of Easterlin's journey he departed the train station late at night, fatigued and concerned about finding his way. He stopped and prayed, asking God to show him the way to the hotel. Before finishing his prayer, he felt a hand on his shoulder. He looked up and saw a man who spoke to him in English and said, "Do you need some help?" He told the man he needed to find his hotel.

"I can help you," the man said. "Come with me." They changed trains three times. The entire time the man didn't speak, remaining still and quiet. After two additional stops they came up out of the subway and the man said "Go two blocks up, turn left, go two more blocks, and the hotel is on the right. Have a good night's rest for your audition. God's blessings are upon you." And then the man quoted the verse, "The LORD thy God is with thee whithersoever thou goest." Easterlin reached for his suitcase and turned to see that the man was gone. He believes to this day that he was in the presence of an angel. He realized that he had never told the man the name of the hotel or the purpose of his trip. If we never stop, we can race past some blessings.

There's another meaningful benefit to keeping spiritual routines that is worth noting, and it brings us back to our beginning. If we make these practices a habit when life is running smoothly and relatively stress free, then they can become especially powerful in moments of unwanted and unexpected crisis—those moments when God truly is waving the red flag.

I recently went through a stressful period that brought my life to a standstill, but my daily habit of scripture reading and prayer was already so ingrained that I never felt tempted to let it drop. Each morning, I sent a distress signal heavenward: *God, please hurry and get rid of these stresses!* On one occasion during my scripture reading, I came across Psalm 62:1: "For God alone my soul waits in silence."

What, I wondered, *could have made the psalmist say that?* As I lingered over the passage, my mind took me to an unexpected place. I found myself recalling an experience that occurred when my three now-grown daughters were youngsters, and I returned home from an out-of-town trip.

Whenever I traveled, I always tried to bring them little gifts so they would know I was thinking of them. When I walked through the door, I loved to hear them shout, "Daddy's home!" and then watch them run to hug me. I would then present them with their gifts.

But one trip, I didn't have a chance to buy them anything. When I walked through the door, the girls came running with their usual excitement and a chorus of "what'd you bring us?" I had to tell them I didn't have gifts.

"But," I said, "I sure am glad to see you!"

My smile was greeted with frowns and shrugs, and the girls went back to the TV. I didn't even get my hugs.

I thought, *So that's how it is. You love and hug Daddy as long as Daddy has something to give you. Why is my presence not enough of a present?*

Now, as I encountered the verse in the psalm, I wondered, *What made me think of that painful episode?* I looked again at the passage, and I tried to connect it to this memory. *Was this really about me and God? Was I most interested in God when I needed something?* In the uncomfortable acknowledgment of that truth, I had to admit that my prayers in recent days had been more about what I wanted God to do. I'd lost sight that I need the Giver more than I need the gifts. I'd also been ignoring all that God was giving me without my asking.

Now God was trying to give me the red flag, but even in my spiritual practice, I resisted taking it. I had been asking God to release me from my stress—and to make it quick. But in this scripture, I could clearly hear God telling me to wait, to rest, and to find that resting place in God. This realization turned my attention to God's provision and helpfulness. By making a simple shift in my focus during prayer and devotion time to God's promises rather than my problems, I let go of wondering if God would show up and do what I needed. I was filled with renewed certainty that God had never abandoned me.

Eventually, my life got back on track. But I know now that I couldn't have taken the green flag again if I hadn't heeded the red one.

Reflection Questions

1. What has happened in your life that felt like a red-flag experience?
2. How do you respond to the statement, "What God does in us while we wait is as important as what it is we are waiting for"?
3. What value does the sabbath have in your life?
4. What pit-stop practices (spiritual habits or disciplines) help you most? What practices would you like to try or learn more about, such as different types of prayer, praying the hours, praying scripture, labyrinth prayer, or fasting?
5. How satisfied are you with your own personal spiritual habits? What, if anything, would you like to change?
6. What do you think is the goal of personal devotional routines?

Notes

⯈⯈⯈ 5

THE BLACK FLAG

When It's Time
to Leave the Race

Mark 9:42-48

Even if you know nothing about racing, you can assume a black flag isn't good. In fact, it's the worst kind of news for a driver: It means *you* are the problem.

The black flag is typically waved at drivers who have mechanical problems or who have violated a rule. Like the blue flag, it is waved at an individual driver, not at the whole field. Unlike the blue flag, though, obeying a black flag is not optional. If you don't leave the race shortly after seeing this flag, then a black flag with a white X comes out, and you're no longer being scored for laps run. The black flag is also called the "consultation flag." This means a racing official has to consult with you about the problem before you can return to the race.

When considering this flag as a spiritual metaphor, I can't help but think of the apostle Paul. You could say his entire ministry started with a black-flag moment. Still known as Saul, he was "breathing threats and murder" against Jesus' disciples (Acts 9:1) when the resurrected Christ met him on the Damascus Road and blinded him. For three pivotal days, Paul had to stop his journey and confront his understanding of God, his own ambition, and the pain he had caused innocent people. When his sight was finally restored, he returned to the "race," but he went in a completely different direction, this time serving Christ.

In our own lives, we experience times when we put ourselves or others in peril. Taking the black flag means we are ready to heed God's signal, to step away, and to break free of what we've been allowing to influence us. Our problem is internal, and it has a name. It's called sin.

Did you cringe? Many people do when they hear the *s* word. "Here you go again, preaching about sin," they say. In their way of thinking, sin belongs to a bygone era and existed to make people feel guilty. People aren't sinners; they just have problems. The church is supposed to lift people up, not make them feel worse about themselves, right?

And yet the issue of sin has a long and revered history. If we feel uncomfortable talking about it, the problem might be that we talk about sin too little in the modern church, not too much.

In her 2001 book *Speaking of Sin: The Lost Language of Salvation*, Barbara Brown Taylor addresses the dis-ease of talking about sin. She draws on the work of Dr. Karl Menninger, the influential psychiatrist and author of the 1973 best seller *Whatever Became of Sin?*

In that book, Menninger ponders whether our modern reluctance to talk about sin has to do in part with the way cultures have historically used sin as a tool for oppression. For instance, antebellum Southerners treated a slave's rebellion as sin; even today, some Christian groups consider the ordination of women to be a sin. "In light of such judgments," Taylor writes, "large numbers of people have simply stopped calling some things sin. The really awful things are turned over to the courts as crimes, while the more self-destructive things are turned over to the medical establishment as mental illnesses, leaving a great deal in the middle to become strictly personal matters."[1]

But like Taylor, I would argue not to throw the baby out with the bathwater. While the concept of sin has been exploited and abused, that doesn't mean it should be retired. As noted theologian Paul Tillich protested in *The Shaking of the Foundations*, "There is a mysterious fact about the great words of our religious tradition: They cannot be replaced. All attempts to make substitutions, including those I have tried myself, have failed to convey the reality that was to be expressed; they have led to shallow and impotent talk."[2]

To retire the word *sin* would ignore a reality that words like *sickness*, *brokenness*, and *failure* don't convey. *Sin* defines a truth about us like no other word.

Digging Deeper into Sin

In chapter 1 I defined sin as separation from God. This definition describes our human condition of alienation from God, from others, and even from the people we ideally want to be. Yet this definition still doesn't capture the full impact of sin. Theologian Walter Brueggemann writes in his book *Genesis*, "Sin is not a breaking of rules. Rather, sin is an aggressive force ready to ambush. . . . Sin is lethal."[3]

Jesus talked about sin this way: "If your hand causes you to fall into sin, chop it off. . . . If your foot causes you to fall into sin, cut it off. . . . If your eye causes you to sin, tear it out" (Mark 9:43-47, CEB). Jesus used the literary device of hyperbole, a statement that purposely exaggerates, like a parent warning a child, "If you do that one more time I'll string you up by your toenails!" It's obvious a parent isn't being literal, but using a grisly image offers a clear warning. In the same way, Jesus was using a painful idea to communicate a perilous truth: Sin is serious business. On another occasion he warned followers not to worry about what can kill the body but what can kill the soul. Jesus talked this way about sin not to make us feel bad but because God doesn't want us to wreck our lives!

Why does talking about sin make us feel bad? Could it be that we equate sinning with being a bad person? If that question hits home, then here is the truth that changes the race: Sin is not the same as bad. Sin makes bad things possible. Recognizing that sin defines us does not diminish the fact that we are also defined by goodness.

Sin can lead to evil. Evil cannot exist without sin. But sin and evil are not the same. Sin is the reality of our incompleteness. We can choose against what is good. That doesn't make us bad. It just means we are . . . faulty.

One time on vacation my wife, Susan, and I were walking back to our hotel, and we came to an intersection. Susan started to turn right, but I said, "We need to go this way," pointing in the opposite direction.

"No," she said, "the hotel is this way."

"My dear wife," I replied with the greatest humility I could muster, "you and I both know who is the directionally challenged one in this relationship. The one thing I never mess up is my sense of direction. The hotel is this way."

"Well," she declared, "if you are so sure, then go that way. But I am going this way." And off she went.

As I watched her walk away, I decided what I would do. I would let her get out of sight and then quietly catch up to her, wait until she realized her mistake, and rescue the damsel in her distress.

How do you think this turned out?

Five minutes later, my mouth fell open as I rounded a corner and found myself staring straight at the hotel. Suddenly I was scared. I was so certain I was right only to discover I was wrong. I had always taken such pride in my sense of direction, and now I realized it had completely failed me. If you can't trust yourself to determine where you should go, then whom can you trust?

This is the problem of sin. Sin confuses our ability to determine right and wrong, good and bad. It doesn't mean we are bad. It just means we can go bad.

An episode from humanity's second generation shows what happens when we discover this lesson the hard way. Consider it the first black flag waved in history.

A Farmer's Black Flag

The Bible first mentions the word *sin* in the story of Cain and Abel, Adam and Eve's two sons. The brothers were very different people, represented by the fact that Cain was a farmer and Abel was a shepherd. One day, each made an offering to God from the fruits of his labor. God looked favorably upon Abel's offering but not upon Cain's. We don't know why. The New Testament indicates Cain didn't offer his gift the right way. (See Hebrews 11:4 and 1 John 3:12.) This interpretation is understandable; otherwise, God appears to be malicious. But Genesis doesn't offer any explanation. It's as if the story is pointing out a truth in life: Not everything is fair. Sometimes people who do the right things in the right way don't always come out on top. And when that happens, we choose our response. Cain decided to get angry.

God reacted with concern. "Why are you angry?" God asked. "And why do you look so resentful? If you do the right thing, won't you be accepted? But if you don't do the right thing, sin will be waiting at the door ready to strike! It will entice you, but you must rule over it" (Gen. 4:6-7). The words hung in the air like a yellow flag; but instead of heeding the warning, Cain acted on his anger and killed his brother.

Seeing this, God asked Cain where his brother was. The question prompted Cain's infamous reply: "Am I my brother's keeper?" The insolence, heaped on the murder, was more than enough for God. The black flag was waved. Abel's blood cried from the ground, God said. Now Cain would be under a curse. His fertile land would turn fallow. Cain would be banished to wander the earth. Sin might not have cost Cain a hand and a foot, but it must have felt that way.

Cain took the black flag. He was removed from the race, and in the "consultation," God issued firm consequences for Cain's actions. But that meant Cain still had an opportunity to go in a new direction, to race again one day.

We all have that chance after the black flag comes out. It all depends on whether we take three important steps.

Step One: Honest Self-Appraisal

Among the Twelve Steps of Alcoholics Anonymous is admitting you are "powerless over alcohol" and making "a searching and fearless moral inventory of yourself." The biblical word for this admission and inventory is *confession*.

When confession is missing, avoidance and denial usually step in, as Cain demonstrated with his retort, "Am I my brother's keeper?"

Without confession we are left to figure out for ourselves how to live with our sin. Either we grow hardened to it, which often encourages repeated bad behavior, or guilt and shame gnaw away at our soul like a corrosive agent. Either way, we don't become better people.

One of my favorite spiritual authors is Frederick Buechner. He has this amazing ability to take ancient spiritual language and concepts and communicate them in fresh, relevant ways. In his book *Beyond Words* he does this with confession. He says, "To confess your sins to God is not to tell God anything God doesn't already know. Until you confess them, however, they are the abyss between you. When you confess them, they become the Golden Gate Bridge."[4]

I love the image of confession as a bridge. It communicates union with God. It says the road continues.

Some years ago I watched a television interview with G. Gordon Liddy and Charles Colson, co-conspirators in the Watergate scandal that eventually led to the resignation of President Richard Nixon. Both Liddy and Colson were convicted for their roles and served prison sentences. After prison, Liddy went on to appear on the lecture circuit and host a political radio talk show. Colson started Prison Fellowship, an international ministry that has brought hope and transformation to hundreds of thousands of inmates, former inmates, and their families.

The interviewer asked both men if they felt they had done anything wrong. Liddy defiantly refused to admit any wrongdoing in Watergate. Colson, however, quickly acknowledged his fault and credited his confession as the starting point of his significant ministry. It built the bridge that allowed the road to continue.

What does it mean when we confess our sins? It doesn't mean self-hatred. It's not beating ourselves up. Confession allows us to retain our goodness while admitting our not-good choices. Confession is also not taking unnecessary blame. Not every sin that affects us is our fault. Confession isn't intended as an exercise of a poor self-image that has us saying, "I'm sorry," at every turn.

Confession begins in a willingness to receive truth. Sometimes that truth comes when we personally acknowledge our actions have hurt others. The more time we spend praying and listening to God, the more open we become to receive what I like to call "stingers of the spirit." One time in my morning prayers, I suddenly got a sick feeling about something I had said in a small group a few days before. I became aware of how my casual words could have hurt a woman in the group. Why this came to me I couldn't explain, but I knew I needed to call her. Sure enough, she admitted to being hurt by what I said. I was able to confess I was careless with my words.

Sometimes the truth comes when other people tell us about our hurtful actions. If we choose to respond with excuses or by insisting the other person is overreacting or hypersensitive, we risk driving a wedge in the relationship. Defensiveness is the enemy of confession. Of course not everything we're accused of is reasonable, but showing an openness to someone else's pain will often get at the truth quicker.

Step Two: Changing Direction

A black flag doesn't go away when we say we are sorry. We also have to repent. That isn't the same thing as regretting our sin. Something has to change. The Greek word for repentance, *metanoia*, actually means to go in a new direction. Without *metanoia,* we are doomed to repeat our mistakes. What brings about different results is to change what brought the bad results.

In racing, a black-flagged car cannot return to the track until the driver has consulted with a racing official. There must be confirmation that the driver has addressed the reason for the black flag. Admission of a problem must result in working to change the problem and going in a new direction.

Cain faced this new direction. It was not an appealing one. Life was going to be very different, but his willingness to change provided hope for a future.

I remember my first black flag that forever changed my direction. I was about four years old. My mother was pushing me in a grocery cart when we passed a shelf with candy. (Interesting how stores put those items right at a kid's eye level.) I was able to reach out and grab the candy, and I asked Mom if I could have it. She said no, took the candy from my hand, and put it back on the shelf.

The rest of the shopping expedition I kept thinking about the candy. I felt wronged for not being allowed to have it. Then we came to the checkout line and what before my wondering eyes should appear, but the same candy! Here was a tremendous life lesson, if I'd been old enough to grasp it: The longer we linger on a sinful act, the less power we have to resist it. When Mom wasn't looking, I grabbed the candy; only this time I kept it secret—until we were in the car headed for home. Sitting in the back seat I brandished my stash so my mother could see it in the rearview mirror.

Now let me say that if repentance is like doing a U-turn, I experienced it with all the speed and skill of Mario Andretti as my mother whirled the large station wagon around to return to the grocery store. My self-satisfied grin faded as we pulled back into the parking lot. My mother took me by the hand into the store and called for the manager. Then she made me hand over the candy and tell him, "This belongs to you. I'm sorry. I stole it."

Up until that moment, I don't think I had ever so willfully defied my mother's judgment. Granted, eating candy is certainly not a sin, but when my mother told me no, I realize now that she was trying to communicate a valuable message: Just because you want something doesn't mean you can have it. She waved a caution flag at me, and still I disobeyed. The black flag came out, and I had to face the consequences.

My return to the scene of the crime actually changed my direction for the rest of my life. That's why I'm so grateful for a mother who would go to the trouble and embarrassment to haul her son in front of a store manager. How easy would it have been for her to think, *I don't have time to drive back to that store. It's just a piece of candy, after all.* She could have lectured me on what I did wrong, but what would I have learned? That I can actually get what I want even when it's not the right way. Instead, without having to use the vocabulary of Genesis, my mother taught me how sin crouches at the door.

Step Three: Starting Over

The process of responding to the consequences of our sin is completed with absolution. God forgives us and releases us from our guilt. Traditional worship liturgies that include a prayer of confession often end with the pastor saying, "In the name of Jesus Christ, you are forgiven," to which the congregation replies with the same words. The repetition affirms that we *all* need forgiveness. Jesus Christ is there to clear us to return to the track. Being removed from the race doesn't mean we will never race again.

When God told Cain the consequences he would face—his new direction—Cain worried, *What if someone comes after me for what I did?"* Cain said, "Anyone who meets me may kill me" (Gen. 4:14, CEB). God replied, " 'It won't happen.' . . . The LORD put a sign on Cain so that no one who found him would assault him" (Gen.

4:15, CEB). From this, we learn grace exists—even for someone who defies God's warning. Cain remained forever marked as God's child, and nothing he or anyone else did could remove that mark. His life would never be the same; he had to pay for what he did. But a black flag didn't disqualify Cain from ever racing again as long as he expressed a willingness to change.

H. Gordon Weekley lived out that truth after he hit his own rock bottom. Back in the 1950s, Weekley was a founding pastor of Providence Baptist Church in Charlotte, North Carolina, one of the fastest-growing churches in America at the time. He was a dynamic, charismatic leader who was loved and respected throughout the Southeast, but he secretly relied on sedatives and amphetamines to help him cope with the demands of his work. His addiction to prescription drugs eventually destroyed his marriage and his ministry.

Yet even in these depths, Weekley discovered God's indelible mark on his life. He joined a 12-step program, accepted God's forgiveness, and got back on his feet. As he healed, he felt called to start a ministry for homeless men called Rebound. Weekley is now deceased, but Rebound fosters his work through the Charlotte Rescue Mission. Weekley's race is over, but his legacy continues to help men who have been black-flagged by addiction and homelessness get back in the race again.

The best of people experience black flags. Moses lost his temper in the wilderness and didn't obey God's instructions. He was black-flagged from entering the Promised Land, yet he is considered the greatest prophet of Israel.

Samson was black-flagged for his continual violations of God's covenant. His long hair, the symbol of God's strength in his life, was cut. Yet his hair grew back, and before he died, he was able to carry out one last courageous act against Israel's enemy.

David had an affair with Bathsheba, another man's wife, and arranged for her husband to fight on the front lines, where he was killed in battle. Yet God declared that the Messiah would come from David's lineage.

Even Cain received his full measure of redemption. After his expulsion, he traveled east of Eden, where he married and had a son. We are told, in fact, of seven generations of sons who came from Cain. Surely the Genesis writer didn't want us to miss the symbolism. The number seven in the Bible represents completeness. Cain took a black flag and still finished his race well.

As awful as sin is, it doesn't sentence us to a life of endless despair. We also have reason to hope. Taking the black flag signals an ending, but it also offers the opportunity for a new beginning.

Reflection Questions

1. What influences and temptations can cause black flags in our everyday lives?
2. What do you think gets lost when we stop talking about sin?
3. How do you reconcile the idea that "sin defines our condition" with the notion that "sin doesn't diminish our goodness"?
4. Catholics consider confession a sacrament and practice it in a formal setting with a priest. If you are not Catholic, how do you incorporate confession into your life?
5. What does it mean to practice repentance, and where does God fit into that practice?
6. If you feel you've had a black-flag experience, how did God prepare you to return to your race of life?

Notes

6

THE WHITE FLAG

Getting in Position
for the Final Stretch

Luke 22:39-46

You don't have to win every time to win . . . depending on what you're trying to win. Make sense?

It does to race-car drivers. In both NASCAR and IndyCar, drivers compete for a points-based championship presented at the end of a season. Points are awarded in each race depending on your position at the finish, number of laps led, and a few other qualifications. In this system a driver could actually win more individual races than anyone else but lose the championship to a driver with more points. You can be the ultimate winner without winning every time.

Life offers us a similar bargain: You don't have to win every argument with your spouse to have a healthy marriage. You don't have to win every debate with your child to be an awesome parent. You don't have to win every time there is a difference of opinion with your coworkers to be an effective employee. You don't have to win every time to win!

In racing, everything comes down to the position you hold in that final lap. The white flag signals this thrilling moment: It appears when the driver in the lead has one lap to go. Even though the white flag is waved for the leader, it's important to all the drivers as they jostle for position. In fact, IndyCar driver Ed Carpenter says he begins a race thinking not about the checkered flag but about the white flag. "Sometimes, depending on the track or situation, I picture being in front," he says, "but most of the time I picture not being first because that will better position me."

If your goal is to win the race, your position will mean one thing, but if your goal is bigger—if it is for the championship—your position might be different. A driver may choose to hold back to secure a fourth-place finish rather than risk getting caught up in a tangle among the leaders.

The same is true for us. Spiritually speaking, the white flag is an invitation to think about how we position ourselves to finish the race well. If we ultimately want healthy relationships, we may have to concede an argument, to let go of control, to give up some of our own desires. If we are never willing to lose anything, we can lose everything. Sometimes we need to surrender.

Surrender. It's a word that brings to mind a different kind of white flag. Picture a Western movie where two cowboys are shooting at each other from behind the rocks. Finally one stops and raises his white kerchief. Losing doesn't sound very appealing, does it? Yet in the last lap of his life, this is exactly what we see Jesus doing.

He endured a kiss of betrayal by his disciple Judas rather than disavow his friendship. He faced arrest rather than hide. He stood silent while on trial rather than defend himself against false accusations. He accepted the brutality of the cross rather than marshal the forces of heaven to fight on his behalf.

The night before his scourging and crucifixion, Jesus needed time to pray so he took his disciples with him to the garden of Gethsemane. Leaving the majority in one spot, he went farther with just a few, and then farther still by himself so that he could be in the company of the only One who could truly help him. His prayer was so intense that Luke described his sweat becoming drops of blood. Finally Jesus said to his heavenly Father, "If you are willing, remove this cup from me; yet, not my will but yours be done" (Luke 22:42).

Jesus entered the last lap of his life in the position of surrender—but it is also how he ran his entire race. We can see this in how he spoke again and again in the language of riddles: "Those who love their life lose it, and those who hate their life in this world will keep it for eternal life" (John 12:25). "Those who find their life will lose it, and those who lose their life for my sake will find it" (Matt. 10:39). "If any want to become my followers, let them deny themselves and take up their cross and follow me" (Matt. 16:24).

What does it mean to follow Jesus in the way of surrender? Make no mistake, what we are talking about here is perhaps as counterintuitive, countercultural, counter-*everything* as anything can get in the spiritual life. What does this kind of "not my will but yours be done" attitude look like day to day? Let's see what it looked like for Jesus in his lifetime.

Surrender Doesn't Mean Giving Up

Jesus' riddles spoke directly to life and death. They were sort of the granddaddy-of-all-statements about losing and gaining. They were also the ones that most confused the disciples, at one point, causing Peter to rebuke Jesus. After hearing Jesus speak of going to Jerusalem to be handed over to the authorities, to be arrested and crucified, and then on the third day to be raised, Peter took him aside to beg him to stop talking this way. (See Matthew 16:21-22.)

There are losses that can't be recouped in the eyes of some. Yet before Jesus was even conceived, Mary was invited by the angel to accept her calling to bear this child by trusting in these words: "Nothing will be impossible with God" (Luke 1:37). Others in scripture were presented with similar tests of faith. When Jesus faced his crucifixion the disciples took their turn. Were they willing to trust Jesus and believe that God would still be able to work—even if the worst thing they could imagine came about?

When we surrender to God's will, we let go of many things: our need to control, our desire to be right, our own vision for how we want life to turn out. But that doesn't mean we give up, especially in our trust in God.

A minister friend of mine tells about a rough period in his life with his rebellious teenage daughter. One Saturday night, he confronted her when she came home under the influence of drugs. After the questioning, arguing, and tears, he stood in the shower at 3 o'clock on a Sunday morning, saying to God, "I have nothing to tell your people today, Lord. I'm just empty."

That week at a visit with the family counselor, the counselor told my friend: "You're just going to have to let go of your daughter." My friend was infuriated. "I thought we were here to work on a new contract, make the expectations clear, and straighten out my daughter," he said. "Understand," the counselor replied, "that doesn't mean giving up. You never give up. But at times, you have to let go and let her find her own way . . . and just keep praying."

As hard as that was, my friend worked at following the counselor's advice. He came to terms with his own limitations. He realized he could love and guide his daughter, but no amount of cross words would compel her to change. Many times he went to prayer, asking for God's help as his daughter went through other painful episodes. Eventually her life turned around. She became an active church member and led a significant outreach ministry. When my friend told me his story, he mentioned that a few days earlier he had undertaken the difficult task of conducting the funeral of a child. After the service, he walked back to his office, where he was surprised to find his daughter. When she told him that she had attended the funeral, he was bewildered. He didn't think she even knew the family.

"I didn't," she said. "I came because I wanted to be here for you, Daddy."

My friend said that years before, he never would have believed that day could be possible. But he had come to understand that surrender doesn't mean giving up. When he finally surrendered his need to control his daughter, both he and she experienced a new life they did not think was possible.

Surrender Means Showing Grace

Several scenes from Jesus' "last lap" stand out as examples of grace and generosity. One occurred in Bethany, where a woman anointed Jesus by pouring an entire jar of expensive perfume on him. Luke (7:36-50) places this story fairly early in Jesus' ministry, but Mark (14:3-9) and Matthew (26:6-13) locate it in the middle of Holy Week shortly before Jesus' arrest and trial. The disciples got into a debate over the wastefulness of the woman's lavish gift, but Jesus chose to focus solely on the woman. He knew her act came from a place of love and gratitude, so he blessed her.

In his darkest hours on the cross, Jesus showed grace to those who reviled him. He prayed, "Father, forgive them." And again, even as he approached his last breath, Jesus was not shielded from a request of need. A thief crucified next to him asked to be remembered when Jesus came into his kingdom. Jesus offered him the gift of "paradise." (See Luke 23:39-43.) In offering this gift, Jesus used an ancient Persian word that means a "walled garden." When a Persian king wished to honor someone, he would invite the person to walk with him in his private garden, thus bestowing friendship. In so many words, Jesus was saying to the repentant thief, "You will walk with me as an honored friend."

Jesus' grand mission of saving the world was always translated into individual opportunities to offer grace. Even on the cross, when it would have been perfectly understandable to abandon his ways, Jesus' attitude and actions didn't change. He noticed others, forgave enemies, and sought to offer comfort. Think about how he positioned himself this way throughout his life. He took children on his knee, talking and listening to them while others tried to convince him he had more pressing business. He heard the cry of two blind men when people said they weren't important enough to merit attention. He saw a funeral procession as a chance to give a widow back her son and raised him from the dead.

How difficult is it for you to surrender to a spirit of grace? When you are in a hurry and the cashier is making mistakes, do you practice patience? When someone is saying unkind, untrue things about you, do you respond with kindness? When you are facing work deadlines and the person next to you appears to be struggling, do you take time to help?

I love the story about three businessmen hurrying to catch the last airport shuttle to make their flight home. While running down the sidewalk, they accidentally knock over a young man's newsstand. Papers and magazines go flying. They all stop to survey the damage, but then they hear the shuttle's horn honk and take off running again. After a few steps, one of the men stops and turns around to help the boy pick up the mess. The other two get ready to board the shuttle and yell back, "Come on or you're gonna miss the flight!" The man just motions for them to go on. Even in his suit, he kneels to help collect and restack all the materials. When they finish, the young man looks up at him and says, "Mister, I wish I had a dad like you."

When we surrender to grace, we often discover the gift of grace for ourselves.

Surrender Means Forfeiting Our Need to Be Right

Jesus frequently urged his disciples to surrender their desire to settle scores, even when they were in the right. "Turn the other [cheek]," he advised (Matt. 5:39). "Pray for those who persecute you," he instructed (Matt. 5:44). "Come to terms quickly," he chided (Matt. 5:25). Then, in the last lap of Jesus' life, his disciples would see him practice what he preached.

When soldiers came to arrest Jesus, Peter cut off the ear of the high priest's servant, but Jesus rebuked him, saying, "He who lives by the sword dies by the sword" (Matt. 26:52). Then Jesus healed the servant. When the frenzied mob shouted, "Crucify, crucify him!" Jesus answered with silence (Luke 23:21). When the religious leaders hurled insults as he hung on the cross, Jesus prayed, "Father, forgive them; for they do not know what they are doing" (Luke 23:34).

Relinquishing the need to get even may be the hardest form of surrendering. Why should I not pursue justice when I know I'm in the right? Because being right may not always offer the best outcome.

Some years ago, I heard another pastor tell about the agony of watching his son's little league all-star game. Though his son had made the team, he happened to play the same position as the coach's son. Guess who sat on the bench?

The pastor realized all parents think their kids are the best players, but in this case he knew it to be true! Yet even in knowing this, he was determined not to be *that* parent, the one who yells his outrage from the stands. He quietly held his disdain in check, until . . .

His son's team had a blowout game. Typically, when that occurs, the coach sends in the reserve players in the final innings. Anticipating this, the pastor kept careful track of the batting order, counting down when his son would be on deck. When the moment arrived, the pastor took to his feet and craned to see, only to watch the coach's son emerge from the dugout with a bat on his shoulder. This was more than the pastor could take. As he headed toward the aisle, he felt his wife's tug on his pants leg knowing it meant, "Please don't embarrass us."

The pastor found a spot where he could peer into the dugout of his son's team, getting as close as he could to see the coach. Fuming, he waited for the coach to look in his direction and notice his glare. But as he stood there, he sensed what he had come to know across the years as God's gentle nudge. The Nudger said, "Go back to your seat." Still, the pastor chose to ignore it. As he waited, though, other forces intervened. The game ended before the coach looked over. The pastor's opportunity to make his point was gone.

Still nursing his grudge, the pastor was humbled by his son's enthusiasm when the boy climbed in the car. "Wow, Dad, we really crushed them, didn't we?" The pastor was proud his son hadn't been soured at all.

That next Sunday, as the pastor got up to preach, he nearly swooned as he looked out and saw the coach and his family in the congregation. They had come to the church for the first time. He knew that had he expressed his anger during the game, this man and his family would not be there that day. Nor would they have returned, as they did, and end up coming to faith in Christ.

Jesus shows us by example the virtue of believing there is a higher calling than simply being right.

Surrender Means Putting Yourself in God's Hands

Finally, the most important action Jesus took in his last lap was to put himself, at all costs, in God's hands. "Not my will, but yours be done," he prayed in the garden of Gethsemane.

But the next day on the cross, Jesus quoted Psalm 22 as he prayed, "My God, my God, why have you forsaken me?" Putting himself in God's hands had not removed the possibility that Jesus would still feel abandoned. In this bleak moment, Jesus identified fully with humanity. To be human is to have times when we question God's fidelity and love. Our experience can include moments of doubt, when we wonder whether God has left us alone.

But then, right before his death, Jesus said, "Father, into your hands I commend my spirit" (Luke 23:46). In the midst of feeling abandoned, Jesus still trusted. These two statements from the cross, which would have been spoken close together, if not in this very order, hold the most powerful tension in all of scripture for me. Can we feel totally abandoned by God and still put ourselves in God's hands?

Even when we find ourselves in a place of complete loss, we can still believe there is a bigger picture. We can let go of our fears and hold on to God's power to do more than we see possible.

In my first appointment as a pastor, I was sent to two small, rural churches in the mountains of western North Carolina. I was twenty-five years old and single, and most of my congregants were retirement age. It was one of the loneliest times of my life. There was no office. No staff. I worked out of my study at home. I bought a dog to keep me company and to give me a reason to get out of bed at a decent hour every morning. I remembered wondering whether I really wanted to be a pastor. *If this is how ministry is going to feel*, I thought, *I'm not sure I'm cut out for it.*

One day I went to see Dr. George Thompson, a pastor who served the largest church in the area. I always found him to be a wise, compassionate man. Over lunch I poured out my struggles, the self-doubt about my call to ministry, and how I was wondering whether I had made the wrong decision. He explained that he viewed his own call to ministry much like he viewed his feelings about marriage. "Some days," he told me, "I wake up and don't feel like being married that day, but my marriage is based on a commitment that's greater than my feelings day to day. My ministry is much like that. I have many days, and sometimes longer periods of my life, when I don't feel like being a minister, but I continue on, because my call is based on God's covenant. It's bigger than feelings."

Moravian missionary Peter Böhler once said to John Wesley, "Preach faith till you have it; and then, because you have it, you will preach faith."[1] Being able to place ourselves in God's hands even as we doubt God requires putting faith before feelings. The disciples encountered this challenge after a day of listening to Jesus offer difficult teachings to a large crowd of followers. Many of his listeners were turned off by the message and chose to part ways. Jesus sensed that the twelve disciples also found his words unsettling; he turned to them and asked whether they also wanted to depart. "Lord, to whom can we go?" Peter responded. "You have the words of eternal life" (John 6:68). The disciples had cast their lot with Jesus. They chose to trust in the hope that had drawn them to Jesus in the first place.

What does that look like for you—to cast your lot with Jesus? What does it mean to put yourself in God's hands even as you're facing into the unknown—or worse, the unwanted?

That was the issue weighing on the woman who came up to me after worship one Sunday. She was distraught over her upcoming move to another city. She was being forced to make the transition for personal reasons, but she felt it was taking her away from God's will for her life.

I listened as she anguished over the move. It was going to erase the way she had pictured her life, she said, and upset all her goals for the future. As she talked, I couldn't help but notice how much she was confusing what she wanted with what God wanted for her. I reminded her that just because she felt she'd lost her direction, that didn't mean God wasn't still her guide. I compared her circumstance to how I use my car's GPS. When I know the way, I don't need it. But every time I'm not sure where to go, I turn to it; it locates me and directs me forward.

Even in a "foreign land," as the psalmist said, this woman needed to know that she could not be removed from God's presence. I suggested she try a "not my will, but yours" kind of prayer modeled after Jesus' prayer in the garden of Gethsemane. She needed to know that she could choose to do God's will wherever she was and trust that by doing that, God would take her where God wanted her to be.

It is a prayer that life requires us to recite again and again. Just as we learned in chapter 1—that accepting Jesus Christ as Lord and Savior isn't something you can do only once—surrender isn't a one-time deal. It's a lap-by-lap effort, and every lap gives us the opportunity to position ourselves for that final sprint to the finish line.

As we conclude this chapter, I invite you to think about where you are in your race of life. Are you in the early stages? Are you midway? Is your race winding down? It's never too soon to think about the position we want to be in when our race finishes. And it's never too late to change positions. For those experienced in the art of spiritual living, surrender is perhaps the most significant act for positioning life for victory. Go ahead. Start right now. Take the white flag.

Reflection Questions

1. When have you found losing to be a winning strategy?

2. At the end of your race, what would you like your life's position to be in terms of financial, relational, and spiritual well-being? What are you doing now to ready yourself for that position?

3. What does the spiritual practice of surrender look like to you in daily living?

4. How do you think surrender is a part of showing grace?

5. How has the need to be right been a problem in your life or the life of someone you love?

6. When have you experienced a moment of surrender when you placed yourself completely in God's hands?

Notes

7

THE CHECKERED FLAG

Experiencing Victory

Luke 24:1-12

Sam Schmidt was a rising star in the IndyCar league when a horrific crash during a 2000 test run left him paralyzed from the shoulders down. Not wanting to give up his passion, he started his own racing team just fourteen months later, and it has become one of the most successful in the sport.

In spring 2014, I met Sam at the Indianapolis Motor Speedway. I'd been told he was in town to test a new car, and I figured that meant a driver from his team would be driving it. Imagine my surprise when I discovered that Sam was the driver! Thanks to technology, he was able to control the car's speed with a mouth stick, and he steered with the help of camera monitors that tracked his head movements; for precaution, an assistant sat in the passenger seat.

I watched in awe as Sam drove several laps, reaching a speed of eighty miles an hour.

I realized how privileged I was to witness this moment. In some ways, it was like Sam had gone from death to life. Fourteen years before, getting behind the wheel of a car again seemed impossible. Yet here he was, testing technology that his team hopes will one day allow quadriplegics to drive.

When Sam pulled off the track and came to a stop just outside the garage, his team surrounded the car, high-fiving one another, taking pictures, and breaking into a huge celebration the world was yet to know about.

As I witnessed the scene, my mind couldn't help but drift to another scene in long-ago Jerusalem where a small, devoted band of followers discovered their own beloved leader had gone from death to life.

On the Friday before their discovery, Jesus' race appeared to be lost. His friends had watched him get arrested and imprisoned. They knew he would be questioned. They hoped that he would just be whipped and released. But by mid-morning those hopes faded when he emerged, bent under the heavy load of a wooden cross. His bloody wounds revealed a savage beating.

By then, most of his party had scattered, but a handful followed his torturous walk to a place called the Skull, where he was nailed to a cross and hoisted up between two thieves who also were being crucified. This man—this good man who loved, healed, forgave, and fed people—was now dying a criminal's death. His diminished entourage watched as he breathed his last and gave up his spirit. Perhaps in that place between denial and shock, they stayed long enough to see his body lowered, wrapped in cloths, and placed in a tomb with a stone sealing the entrance. That was it. Their friend, their Lord, Jesus, was dead.

Then, on the third day, a Sunday, women who were followers of Jesus went to the tomb to embalm his body with burial spices, a ritual they were unable to perform immediately after his death. It was one last act of devotion they could show. Imagine their shock when they found the stone rolled away and two angels who asked them: "Why do you look for the living among the dead?" (Luke 24:5). The women couldn't fathom the question. They weren't looking for the living among the dead. They were looking for the dead!

On Easter morning the angels raised a rhetorical question because they already knew what the women would soon discover. Jesus had been resurrected. He was among the living once again.

The angels' question continues to resonate through the ages. Indeed, can we find the living even among the dead? Can we find victory even in the face of undeniable defeat?

For Christians, Easter is our checkered flag—our victory flag. To be sure, it is victory over universal forces, such as sin, injustice, and evil. But Jesus' victory over death has an individual, personal impact as well. Easter is a present experience. It signals the way to hope amid pain, suffering, and despair. It means new life can be ours through faith. How does that happen? What can Easter teach us about experiencing victory?

Living with Victory Is More Than Blind Optimism

The way some people talk about "living with victory" can make others just roll their eyes. Even though some life situations don't invite a bright side, these rosy optimists still try to find one. They talk about victorious living as if all we have to do is picture what we want to happen and *voila!*—much like Dorothy closing her eyes, clicking her heels, and reciting, "There's no place like home."

Still others turn victorious living into a kind of spiritual manipulation. I recently heard about a group of Christian college students who were driving to an event when they realized they were about to run out of gas. Not having the money to buy more, they pulled over and prayed for God to allow them to get to their destination with the gas they had on hand. I'm not saying that a nearly empty gas tank is too much for God to handle, but I do believe that God may favor planning ahead!

So let's turn to the women who went to the tomb that first Easter morning. There was no saccharine optimism on their part. They didn't go thinking, *We've spent the whole night asking God to do something big, so that's what we expect to find.* They were grounded in the crushing reality of their situation, yet they were still determined to go on living.

How could they do both?

In his best-selling business book *Good to Great*, Jim Collins offers some insight into that question with what he calls the Stockdale Paradox. It's named after US Admiral James Stockdale, who spent eight years as a prisoner of war in the notorious "Hanoi Hilton" during the height of the Vietnam War. As the commanding officer,

Stockdale doggedly rallied the other American POWs to resist their captors' propaganda techniques, survive deprivation and torture, and muster strength among their haggard ranks. Stockdale himself endured over twenty episodes of torture that left him with permanent injuries. He did this not knowing if he would ever be freed or even if he would survive.

Of course, by the time Collins caught up with Stockdale many years later, the whole world knew Stockdale's outcome. He was released in 1973 to a hero's welcome, and he went on to receive the Congressional Medal of Honor for his bravery. But Collins came to Stockdale because he wanted to understand how he dealt with the trials of imprisonment without knowing the end of the story.

Collins first asked Stockdale about the POWs who didn't survive their ordeal, and Stockdale said they fell into a single category: "The optimists." He went on to explain that these men pinned their fate on target dates—hoping they would be released by Easter or Thanksgiving or Christmas. "And Easter would come, and Easter would go," Stockdale explained. "And then Thanksgiving, and then it would be Christmas again. And they died of a broken heart."

Then Stockdale identified the paradoxical mind-set that allowed him to survive the most merciless conditions. "This is a very important lesson," he said. "You must never confuse faith that you will prevail in the end—which you can never afford to lose—with the discipline to confront the most brutal facts of your current reality, whatever they may be."[1]

Collins considers this "unifying concept" to be a "signature of all those who create greatness, be it in leading their own lives or in leading others." In spiritual terms, I consider it victorious living.

Stockdale didn't indulge in blind optimism. Nor did the women at the tomb. They fully grasped their situation, and yet they didn't give in to despondency. By letting go of old hope, they were unknowingly ushering in new hope. The God who said, "Behold, I make all things new" (Rev. 21:5, KJV), also said, "Do not remember the former things, or consider the things of old" (Isa. 43:18).

God can do better than renew: God can resurrect. Easter Sunday doesn't happen without Good Friday. Resurrection is the offspring of death. When we are willing to accept death, resurrection becomes a possibility.

There's another critical aspect of the women's story that leads to the experience of celebration and victory. Notice that they went to the tomb to prepare the body with burial spices. Despite their sorrow, they were intent on carrying out this act of devotion.

Think about the many spiritual disciplines that can become rote: attending worship and other religious events, praying regularly, studying scripture. Sometimes these activities are hard, not because they are demanding but because we lack motivation. Have you ever found that you need all the energy you can muster just to get out of bed and go to church on Sunday morning? Some weeks that happens even to pastors!

Perhaps you practice acts of devotion that require both strength and desire. You may volunteer to serve meals in a soup kitchen, visit in a nursing home, or tutor at-risk students. Inspiration helps when you're doing these sorts of tasks. But what if you don't feel inspired?

Think again about the women in the Easter story, and imagine how easy it would have been for them to stay home that day. But they didn't, and they found a miracle.

If we too act in faith, even when we've lost hope, can God help restore our hope?

God Works Even When We're Not Looking

It's worth noting that none of the Gospel accounts explains how the Resurrection took place. The writers say nothing about how the stone was rolled away or what happened to bring Jesus to life. Did his heart just begin beating and his other organs gradually restart? Did his whole body go through a metamorphosis of some kind? Did this miracle occur instantly or over a period of several hours?

None of these questions is answered by the Easter story because there were no witnesses. The women at Jesus' tomb discovered the living among the dead. The message is that God is at work even when we can't see God in action. God continues doing something even when we believe God is done. Most important, the Easter story communicates that we don't have to understand how God works to experience God working.

Think about it: Sometimes the most profound act of faith comes in refusing to give up on God—then waiting to see what God can accomplish. Returning to worship after experiencing a bitter tragedy could lead us to new healing. Serving others or giving generously even when we're mired in cynicism could lead us to a spiritual breakthrough. Committing to religious practice even when we feel God has let us down could lead us. . . . Well, let a guy named Bucky tell you what can happen.

Bucky had a rough childhood. His parents separated when he was seven years old. He stayed with his mother, who became an abusive alcoholic. When Bucky was fourteen, she kicked him out of the house. On the streets, he discovered a tremendous gift: manipulation. He could tell people what they wanted to hear, and in turn they would do his bidding. He used flirtation to con women into giving him a place to stay. He lied to people to get money and other favors. He also began using drugs. By age seventeen, he was serving a six-month prison sentence.

A couple of years after his release, Bucky met Brooke, a young woman who happened to be the daughter of the music director at my church. While Brooke was falling in love with Bucky, he saw Brooke as someone who could serve his purposes. Using his gift of manipulation, he talked her into marrying him, but his lifestyle didn't change all that much.

Bucky's first crisis of faith arrived when the couple had a baby who became critically ill just days after his birth. Actually, up to this point, you wouldn't exactly say Bucky had a faith. When relatives and friends talked with him about turning things over to God, he would think to himself, *Just how do I do that? God is someone I can't see, who doesn't listen to me, and who sure doesn't answer back.* Yet with his son so sick, Bucky tried talking to God. He asked that his son be spared. But when the baby died two weeks after his birth, it further confirmed for Bucky that faith was a hoax.

Doctors determined Bucky and Brooke both carried a gene that had passed a rare disorder on to their son. Eventually, the couple turned to *in vitro* fertilization to create embryos that could be screened for the gene. But the implants failed. Brooke kept miscarrying.

The disappointment took a toll on the couple's marriage. Bucky became reckless, relying more and more on his selfish impulses. After one too many lies, Brooke finally had enough and left him. Bucky was shocked. For the first time in his life he couldn't manipulate someone to do what he wanted. No amount of words, attention, or false kindness could win Brooke back. He even resorted to coming to church. Obviously desperate times call for desperate measures!

One Easter Sunday, Bucky found me after the final worship service of the day and asked if we could talk. I was exhausted from the morning's schedule, not to mention hesitant. My few previous encounters with Bucky had not impressed me. I knew he had not been good to Brooke. He had treated me with complete disinterest, as if getting too close might infect him with something he didn't want. But I agreed to listen, and he poured out his story through his tears.

If I'd known about his upbringing, I might have shown him more grace than I did. Instead, I was just weary enough to tell him what I really thought, "Bucky, if you are here to try to win back Brooke, forget about it. In fact, I hope you don't. She deserves better. You have treated her lousy and have been a sorry husband. But today is Easter, and I believe new life is possible—but only if you want it. Don't choose that if you are just trying to manipulate Brooke into taking you back. You need to let her go and focus on getting your life together. At some point you need to turn your life over to God and see what God can do with you because your choices obviously haven't turned out so well." Then we prayed, and he headed out the door. I honestly assumed I would never see Bucky again—certainly not the next Sunday!

But there he was, wearing a dress shirt and sitting in a pew. In fact, over the coming weeks, he was in church every Sunday. We continued our conversations about faith and what it means to put yourself in God's hands. Though I can't quite describe it, Bucky gradually began to look different to me. There was something about his humility, his gentleness, his appreciation. He would later say that during this time, worshiping every Sunday, he began to feel God becoming real to him. He knew he had to let go of Brooke. For the first time in his memory, he wasn't motivated by his own needs. Instead, he thought about Brooke—what she needed and deserved—and he came to the painful admission that it wasn't him! He wanted her to find happiness and someone who would treat her the way she deserved. Eventually, he said to God, "Okay, Lord, I tried living on my own and doing things my way and that obviously hasn't turned out well so I want to do it your way." The following Sunday, Bucky came to me before one of the services and asked if I would baptize him that morning. What a special day it was . . . one of many.

About six months after Bucky's Easter visit to me, he and Brooke began talking again. She too discovered the transformation I'd seen in Bucky, and they decided to try pressing the "restart" button. They began going out on dates. One thing led to another, and they became a couple again. Though they were still legally married, they wanted to do something that signified their new life together, so they decided to renew their wedding vows. Bucky said it was really the first wedding for him, because this time he honestly meant he would love, honor, and cherish his wife.

A few years later, with their marriage on solid ground, Bucky and Brooke decided to try *in vitro* fertilization again with the healthy embryos they still had stored. But this time, Brooke learned she had developed health issues that meant she couldn't carry a baby. Just at the moment they were ready to give up, Brooke's sister came to them and said she had felt God telling her that she was to carry their child. After several months of tests and preparation, the sister began a successful pregnancy with one of the embryos.

On May 1, 2015, a baby girl was born to Bucky and Brooke. Just when you feel all hope is lost, God reminds you that you are not forgotten.

Neither Bucky nor I could ever have imagined these possibilities on that Easter when he first spoke to me, but because he chose to practice devotion, it led to new life . . . literally a new, young, beautiful, healthy life.

Hope Is Meant to Be Passed On

Finally, let's consider one more aspect of the Easter story and what it teaches us about experiencing victory and the checkered flag. Look at the response of the women after their encounter with the angels at the empty tomb. "They left the tomb quickly with fear and great joy, and ran to tell his disciples" (Matt. 28:7-8). The women became messengers of hope. They couldn't wait to share their discovery. They had something to tell. This image of the women running to tell the disciples reveals how God relies on people to convey hope to others.

A couple years ago, my church learned about a horrific tragedy in our city. A single mother had lost two of her four children in a condo fire, and she had suffered severe injuries. At the time, the family was already in the process of taking ownership of a home donated through

Habitat for Humanity, but the house still needed about $20,000 in repairs. Now the family was in even more desperate need of this new home. Could my congregation rise to the challenge to help?

On an Easter Sunday, church members gave above and beyond this amount—and that was on top of the regular offering! Besides the financial support, they also volunteered to do the renovation work. Nothing could replace the loss this mother had experienced, but we could offer comfort and hope in the midst of the hurt. Goodness abounded in people coming together to surround this mother and keep her from facing such heartache alone. Victorious living comes not from what others do for us but from what we share with others. In giving hope, we received hope in return.

The Essence of Faith

In the world of NASCAR and IndyCar, the checkered flag signals that the race has been won, and in this book, I've made several references to finishing your race well. Yes, if we're fortunate enough to have the opportunity to look back at the end of our lives, we want to be able to claim victory. What will success mean for you? What do you want your most meaningful relationships to look like when the checkered flag comes down? What accomplishments will mean the most to you? If other people consider you a champion, what will make them feel that way?

While it is important to consider those outcomes, God assures us there is something of even greater value: Our victory isn't dependent on the outcome.

Look back on some of the stories you've read in this chapter. You've met a quadriplegic who was able to drive a test car, a wayward husband who healed his marriage and improbably welcomed a baby, the victim of a house fire who received a new home, and the women at a tomb who encountered a risen Christ.

Each of these stories is immensely reassuring. Observed in hindsight, they offer satisfying, even miraculous, outcomes. That's the way we want all of life to turn out, isn't it? But here's the rub. We also know life doesn't always turn out that way.

Over the years, I've often counseled people as they go through desperate circumstances. The same question has been put to me time and again: What good is faith if it doesn't seem to change the outcome of my struggle?

It's an honest question that springs from grief and pain and disappointment, but I also believe it misses the point about faith. Faith isn't about making God a magic genie to do our bidding. Faith shouldn't depend on getting our way.

What good is faith? It holds the power to bolster our spirit. It offers us a sense we're not enduring our struggles alone. It provides us with strength and courage that is not our own. It gives us an active role in God's greater purpose. And it promises us a hope for the future, whatever the future holds.

Consider the moment in each of those four stories when the people were in the depths of their despair. Think about Sam Schmidt after his accident, certain he would never drive again. And Bucky, when he realized he'd destroyed his marriage. Imagine the fire victim grieving over the loss of her home and two children, and the women who watched their beloved friend die on a cross.

At these lowest moments, none of these people could have possibly imagined a glimmer of the outcomes that awaited them. But that is what God offers us: the promise of the unimaginable.

Hope is too easy to abandon when all seems lost. But living with hope is the essence of faith. That means we don't have to wait until the end of the race to experience victory. We can seize it every day when we choose to live with hope. Go ahead, live victoriously each and every day. Take the checkered flag.

Reflection Questions

1. What feelings do you have as you imagine walking with the women to the tomb that first Easter morning?

2. How have you had to practice the "Stockdale Paradox"—when you had to hold on to hope while facing brutal facts?

3. When have you been tempted to give up on God?

4. What are you doing in your life right now to give hope to others?

5. What value do you find in faith if it doesn't necessarily change the outcome of your struggles?

6. What does victorious living look like to you?

Notes

ACKNOWLEDGMENTS

Take the Flag is not just a book; it is a DVD small-group companion, study guide, children's and youth material, publicity program and more! Much credit and thanks go to the many behind-the-scenes people who not only lent a hand but also made these pieces come together.

I first want to express my appreciation to publisher Sarah Wilke, book marketing and sales director Janice Neely, and all The Upper Room's great staff for their vision to take on such a unique project. I'm especially grateful to project manager Betsy Hall for her immense patience and skill in coordinating so many pieces. Her diligent, roll-up-your-sleeves work ethic is the reason this project made it to completion.

I'm equally indebted to Nancy Kruh, an outstanding editor I am also fortunate to call my sister-in-law. This was our first project together, and I cannot express enough appreciation for her gentle, helpful coaching, as well as her persistent prodding to meet deadlines and complete assignments. Most of all, I am grateful for her commitment to do whatever it takes, including an eleventh-hour trip to Indianapolis to hammer out the final chapters.

Of course, without my wife, Susan, this book would not exist. Her encouragement to turn a sermon series into a resource is what led to this product. She read and reread each chapter, offering insightful suggestions and encouragement. She also wrote the small-group guide that will make this book a truly transformational resource. My three daughters, Julie, Sarah, and Anna, have been gracious to allow me to use their experiences in sermons, and now books, as their childhoods keep getting relived long after they've grown up.

Further thanks go to my executive assistant, Marsha Thompson, whose work lining up interviews with racing personalities was crucial to the creation of the DVD companion. Her tenacity and can-do attitude are a joy to work with every day.

I'm also grateful to my friends Ron Pegram, former Motor Racing Outreach (MRO) chaplain, and his wife, Jackie, for helping make contacts in NASCAR circles. Current MRO chaplain Nick Terry also helped us connect with a number of people and offered good advice about locations and times for interviews. On the Indy-Car side, gratitude goes to my dear friend and church member Tom Godby for his help contacting drivers.

Of course, I can't overstate my appreciation for all the drivers and crew team members who gladly consented to be interviewed for this project. They gave generously of themselves, and their personal stories have enlivened this book and turned the DVD into a rich resource. I particularly want to mention Caron Myers for her enthusiastic support for this work and her help in making contact with racing personalities and venues. Sam Hornish Jr. also reached out to colleagues on my behalf; he is a wonderful servant of Christ whom I have been honored to get to know through this experience. I am also deeply grateful to Matthew Pessoni and the team at Gemini Production Group who were a pleasure to work with. Also, I want to thank Brian Annakin and his team at IMS Productions. Brian has become a friend going back to his help with the sermon series. With his work on the DVD, he once again has gone above and beyond the call of duty.

Finally, I want to thank two churches, in my past and present, where *Take the Flag* took shape. The congregation of Williamson's Chapel United Methodist Church in Mooresville, North Carolina, is where I first preached a series using the flags in racing and began thinking about creating this book and resource. I want to specifically mention my colleague from that church, Mark Jordan, whose encouragement was fuel in the tank. Shake and bake, my friend!

Most especially I am grateful to the congregation I now serve, St. Luke's United Methodist Church in Indianapolis, for their support in giving me time to write and travel to produce *Take the Flag*. I also want to offer my indebtedness to the pastors and staff of St. Luke's for shouldering the extra burden my time away put on them. It is a privilege to serve such a unique and dynamic church.

NOTES

1. The Green Flag

1. Fil Anderson, *Running on Empty: Contemplative Spirituality for Over-achievers* (Colorado Springs, CO: WaterBrook, 2005), 65–66.

2. Bob Dylan, "Gotta Serve Somebody," *Slow Train Coming*. New York, NY: Columbia Records: 1979.

2. The Yellow Flag

1. *Days of Thunder*. Directed by Tony Scott. Hollywood, CA: Paramount Pictures, 1990.

2. Tiger Woods's Feb. 19, 2010, statement. www.cnn.com/2010/US/02/19/tiger.woods.transcript/

3. Harry Emerson Fosdick, *Riverside Sermons* (New York, NY: Harper & Brothers Publishers, 1958), 83–93.

3. The Blue Flag

1. *Talladega Nights: The Ballad of Ricky Bobby*. Directed by Adam McKay. Culver City, CA: Sony Pictures, 2006.

2. Stephen R. Covey, *The 7 Habits of Highly Effective People: Powerful Lessons in Personal Change* (New York, NY: Free Press, 1989), 30–31.

3. Barbara Glanz, *Care Packages for the Workplace: Dozens of Little Things You Can Do to Regenerate Spirit at Work* (New York, NY: McGraw-Hill Education, 1996), 139–40.

4. The Red Flag

1. John Ortberg, *If You Want to Walk on Water, You've Got to Get Out of the Boat* (Grand Rapids, MI: Zondervan, 2003), 178.

2. Marva J. Dawn, *Keeping the Sabbath Wholly: Ceasing, Resting, Embracing, Feasting* (Grand Rapids, MI: Eerdmans Publishing, 1989), 65–66.

3. Henri J. M. Nouwen, *Out of Solitude: Three Meditations on the Christian Life* (Notre Dame, IN: Ave Maria Press, 2004), 25.

5. The Black Flag

1. Barbara Brown Taylor, *Speaking of Sin: The Lost Language of Salvation* (Lanham, MD: Cowley Publications, 2001), 23.

2. Paul Tillich, *The Shaking of the Foundations* (Eugene, OR: Wipf and Stock, 2012), 153–54.

3. Walter Brueggemann, *Genesis,* Interpretation: A Bible Commentary for Teaching and Preaching (Louisville, KY: Westminster John Knox, 1982), 57.

4. Frederick Buechner, *Beyond Words: Daily Readings in the ABC's of Faith* (San Francisco, CA: HarperOne, 2004), 65.

6. The White Flag

1. John Wesley, March 4, 1738, *Journal and Diaries* I (1735–1738), ed. W. Reginald Ward and Richard P. Heitzenrater, vol. 18 of *The Bicentennial Edition of the Works of John Wesley* (Nashville, TN: Abingdon Press, 1976), 228.

7. The Checkered Flag

1. Jim Collins, *Good to Great: Why Some Companies Make the Leap . . . and Others Don't* (New York, NY: HarperBusiness, 2001), 83–87.

ABOUT THE AUTHOR

Rob Fuquay serves as senior pastor at St. Luke's United Methodist Church in Indianapolis, one of the largest churches in the denomination. Before taking this pulpit in 2011, he served several congregations, both large and small, in his native North Carolina. Rob earned his undergraduate degree from Pfeiffer College (now University) in Misenheimer, North Carolina, and his master of divinity from Candler School of Theology at Emory University in Atlanta. He loves the outdoors and enjoys hiking, climbing, and playing golf. Rob and his wife, Susan, also are sports fans who avidly follow baseball, football, basketball, and of course, auto racing. They are the parents of three daughters, Julie, Sarah, and Anna. Rob's previous study series, the best-selling *The God We Can Know*, was released by Upper Room Books in 2014. To learn more about Rob and his published works, visit robfuquay.com.